THE LIFE OF
THE WHITE ANT

Photograph: Victor Wolfgang von Hagen

A CARTON NEST OF NASUTITERMES ATTACHED TO A TREE IN THE JUNGLES OF ESMERALDAS IN WESTERN ECUADOR. THE NEST WEIGHS 200 POUNDS AND CONTAINS APPROXIMATELY 3,000,000 INDIVIDUAL INSECTS

THE LIFE OF THE
WHITE ANT

BY
MAURICE MAETERLINCK

TRANSLATED BY
ALFRED SUTRO

WITH A PREFACE
AND ILLUSTRATIONS FROM PHOTOGRAPHS BY
VICTOR WOLFGANG von HAGEN

NEW YORK
DODD, MEAD & COMPANY
1939

PRINTED IN THE UNITED STATES OF AMERICA
BY THE VAIL-BALLOU PRESS, INC., BINGHAMTON, N. Y.

THE Translator wishes to express his indebtedness to Mr. J. F. E. Scanlan for much valuable assistance

PREFACE

Last year termites destroyed over 40,000,000 dollars worth of property in the United States alone. This destruction was not catastrophic; there was no spectacular collapsing of buildings, no visible army conducting systematic depredations, rather the pyramiding damage was carried on clandestinely, cryptically, almost imperceptibly by blind, soft-bodied insects, popularly, but erroneously known as "White Ants."

This is not a new invasion of the White ants. There is not, as has been often suggested, a sudden incursion of new types of these voracious termites, but simply the adjustment to Man of those species who have been living here for millions of years before Man entered upon the American scene.

The present termite problem has arisen merely because Man has attempted to change the ordinary processes of nature by trying to conserve as his own, over a protracted period of time, wood and its cellulosic by-products, which the termites regard as their substance to consume, break down into basic chemical elements, and convert into humus which in turn is utilized by growing vegetation. Thus it is that Man and the termite have come to grips. Unfortunately for us, the termite has not been able to differentiate between "types" of dead vegetable matter and finds the joists of our homes, the books on our shelves and the stamps in the postoffices just as toothsome morsels as the dead trees on the prairies. Nor is the termite to blame, for we have built great concentrations of wooden structures over parts of the earth which have been a habitat of termites for millions of years.

It took us some little time to discover that the millions of dollars of damage annually caused by the termites was not a momentary caprice of nature, but was perpetrated by a group of tenacious, although fragile insects, held together by an amazing social organization, which ceaselessly carved away with sharply dentated mandibles at the very bastions of our social structures. For many years the investigation of the termite realm was properly left in the hands of the entomologist who looked upon this primitively constructed insect mostly as an extraordinary biological phenomena. The entomologist, however, never failed to insist that the destruction of our buildings was not being caused by dry rot in defective wood, but by termites, generally the common damp-wood termite, *Reticulitermes,* which must maintain contact with the soil (thus building earthen tubes through which to reach its feeding grounds) as well as another type, the *Kalotermes,* which were able to live without this ground contact. It was emphasized that only through a profound knowledge of the insects' habits, would Man be able to control them. When the cost of the termites' depredations reached astronomical proportions, when the damage caused by their infestations was topped only by fire-damage; then only did we systematically begin to attack the termite problem. In order, adequately, to cope with it, entomologists, biologists, toxicologists, foresters, chemists, structural engineers, cooperated in an attempt to solve the termite problem, and to contribute their part to it. In fact no system of termite control has been successful that has disregarded the various technological fields which the termite entered when it began to undermine our structures. Since no untreated wood is termite-proof (the sales talks of the lumberman notwithstanding), many involved experiments in chemically impregnating wood were undertaken, which would make it impervious to the voracious cellulose appetites of termites and at the same time, would not leech out under the soil. Control, too, centered about the most efficacious manner of placing wood in the structure of buildings so that termites could not easily use it. Further, there were extensive experiments with the habits of termites in order to search out the weakest link in the chain of insect behavior to prevent, not only the further developing of each particular termite colony, but at the same time lessening potential infestations arising from each colony. Thus it is that this little insect has brought about a vast industry of chemically-treated woods, exterminators and technicians who must realize that there is no one panacea for the termite problem but that the whole is bound up with a strict adherence to, first, the actual structure of the building, and, secondly, a continual inspection and maintenance to prevent new termite infestations.

The termite as a social group is very ancient. Of the eighteen hundred known species of termites that cover the earth as many as fifty-eight are to be found in North America—an unusually large termite-fauna for a non-tropical region. Of these termites that we harbor, a large percentage are of economic significance and are truly American. For fossil termites have been found in the Florissant beds of Colorado which are structurally so similar to the present-day termite that it is evident that the termite has been in its North American habitat for millions of years. Fossil termites are also present in Baltic amber, the kind found in North Prussia. Since amber is merely the fossiled resin of pines which flourished during the Oliogocene Tertiary, its viscidity imprisoned the winged termites of those pre-historic times and brought them down to us so well preserved that we are able to compare them with the termites that haunt us today. There has been very little change in these insects throughout all these millions of years. The conclusion is inescapable that the termite had ages ago perfected its social organization and has been more or less marking time for the last 50,000,000 years. The specialization of termites since they evolved from a primitive form of cockroach—*Protoblattoids*—to be technical—has been a one-sided progress, as all specialization is apt to be, and the termite has undoubtedly reached a certain biochemical limit in the perfection of its curious society.

But the specialization of the individuals of this "society" into distinct castes is so ultra-human . . . a fact that M. Maeterlinck brings out so very well . . . and has produced a cooperative communism so final, that most radical Soviets would in comparison be conservative capitalists.

Assume that Roy Chapman Andrews returned home from one of his explorations and reported that he had found a race of people who could control not only the sex of the various castes of their society, but the bodily structure as well; that to defend their realm they had perfected a blind soldier caste— a warrior who bears his weapons on his head, yet could not eat and was dependent on the worker caste—another blind apterous caste-member. This worker bears the brunt of enlarging the realm, feeds all its inhabitants, yet has little or nothing to say as regards the structure of the society. And, finally, a hierarchy of reproductives, a caste of fertile kings and queens, who alone repopulated the realm, who kept their other prospective reproductives in check by subtly exuding an inhibiting substance from their bodies which, lapped eagerly up by the supplementary queens, caused them to remain sterile, thus chemically regulating the production of the quasi-fertile castes. Would not all this be unbelievably fantastic?

Yet, one need not go to the Gobi Desert for such a race; you may have them in your own backyard, your cellar, in the very chair on which you are sitting. You may live for months, years, in the midst of termites without setting eyes on a single individual, so carefully do they remain in the crypts they have carved in the wood that we wish to preserve. You know nothing of them until a table collapses, the piano leg enters what appears to be a sound floor, or an agent of the Federal Housing Administration denies you a loan because you have termites. It is then that you turn a willing ear to termite "exterminators"; only to learn after multiple treatments that the termites cannot, like the true ant, be exterminated by placing sweetened poison in strategic places.

When you mention that there are *White Ants* in your house, you will be scornfully told by the specialists—who will insist that this insect is neither white nor an ant—that this popular name complicates the control, since the habits of the termites are vastly different from those of the true ant. What one has, if one's house is being eaten away, are termites. If the layman then wishes to admonish the scientists in turn he may, on inquiry, learn that the name termite is almost as ridiculous as "white ant." For it was derived by Linnaeus, the Swedish systematist, from the Greek word *Terma*—the goal, or end of life. Linnaeus confused the termite with the death watch beetle, a species of the *Anobiidae,* that eats the wood of old furniture.

Preface

This beetle has a curious sexual phase, a mating habit of knocking its head against wood, giving out a faint ticking sound. To the superstitious European peasant this was a sign that presaged death: thus the name death watch beetle. Confusing bodies of the "White Ant" and the beetle created for the former the absurd name of term-ite, which with this insect's extravagant fertility, is hardly a suitable symbol of death.

One may well wonder if the scientists are not themselves indulging in a bit of anthropomorphic leg-pulling when they refer to a "termite society."

What sort of "social life" can blind, minute, soft-bodied insects possess? How can these primitive insects, certainly not much more than unreasoning automata, have developed a society so compact that it has withstood all of Man's efforts to eradicate?

One makes inquiries at libraries about the literature on termites and finds it is relatively scarce. Pamphlets and books on the subject are highly technical or else written in a style at once so tough and plodding that the books tell the amateur investigator, as a boy once remarked of a book about penguins, more about termites than he wants to know.

Anyone who has not been put off by the first dull fare will with delight come across "The Life of the White Ant" by M. Maurice Maeterlinck. Here one will find what one is seeking. This book gives the factual material on the lives of these amazing insects, while at the same time there is sprinkled between the facts, like the sugar coating on a bitter pill, mystical speculations by M. Maeterlinck and bits of philosophical deductions, which cannot help stimulating the reader.

In writing this book, in a sense a companion piece to "The

Preface

Life of the Bee," yet at the same time so antithetical, M. Maeterlinck drew his information from some of the foremost in-
vestigators of his time including the remarkable work of Dr.
Cleveland of Harvard University with his fascinating experiments on the intestinal hosts of termites.

Since "Life of the White Ant" was written (1925) the investigations of the biology of termites have taken remarkable
strides forward in an interpretation of their habits. Many of
us interested in this remarkable insect have entered the forests
of the Amazon, the veldts of Africa, to secure new specimens
and to search out some of the inextricable points of their behavior.

As a naturalist, I might take exception to the mystical course
of M. Maeterlinck's deductions, founded even as they are on
the best of sources, on his theories about the unseen powers that
operate the termitary and the relatively human terms that he
gives to the actions of termites. We have come to feel that we
are not dealing with a wholly mystical animal, but with one
that is understandable within the realms of our own intelligence; that the behavior of termites is made up of "apetitive or
aversive cycles," of hunger, of sex, repeated many times over
during the life cycles of the insect, so that the whole of these
apetitive cycles becomes a very elaborate pattern which we call,
for lack of another name—instincts. But instinct is not unerr-
ing as Fabre and Maeterlinck believe. Like intelligence, with
which it is sometimes juxtaposed, it can do some very stupid
things. But these are insignificant quibblings. In the "Life of
the White Ant," we have, with few exceptions, the only available life of these insects written in a form that a non-specialist
may enjoy.

Preface

After all, the end of any science, objective or subjective, is Man. In order for the average man to understand and appreciate the habits of anything not wholly human they must be described in such terms that they bear a relation to himself. If such be called "popularization" or "anthropomorphization," it matters little, so long as it serves its purpose of awakening, stirring in man a curiosity of the ways of Nature. And the "Life of the White Ant," by M. Maeterlinck, does precisely that.

VICTOR WOLFGANG VON HAGEN
Fellow of the Zoological Society of London

Berkeley, California
May, 1939

CONTENTS

ILLUSTRATIONS

I
INTRODUCTION

I

INTRODUCTION

I

*T*HE *Life of the White Ant* does not, any more than *The Life of the Bee,* belong to the school of romantic biography that is so popular to-day. The accuracy of every statement in the earlier work has been admitted by the specialists, and I have remained faithful to the principle which guided me before: I have steadfastly resisted the temptation to enhance the marvel of reality by adding marvels that may be attractive but are not true. Being older, I have found the temptation less; for, little by little, the years teach every man that truth alone is marvellous. Another thing that they teach an author is that embellishments are the first of all to fade, that they age more quickly than he; and that only facts strictly set forth, and reflections that are precise and sincere, will present the same appearance to-morrow as they do to-day.

I have therefore not stated a fact or reported an incident that is not indisputable or cannot be easily verified. This is one's first duty when dealing with a world so unfamiliar and disconcerting as the one we are about to enter. The most innocent fancy, the slightest exaggeration, the least inaccuracy, would deprive a work of this kind of all credibility and interest. I hope I have made no such mistake, although on some points, perhaps, I may have been led into error by my authorities;

and yet this is not very likely, for I have taken into account the works of professional entomologists only, purely objective and dispassionate writers, solely concerned with scientific observation. These writers, as a rule, seem scarcely to appreciate the extraordinary nature of the insect they are studying; and, in any case, show not the least anxiety unduly to dwell upon this, or to exaggerate it.

I have borrowed very little from the narratives of the hundreds of travellers who have described the white ant or termite; they are generally unreliable, for they will either give unverified stories related to them by the natives or add embroidery of their own. The only exception I have made to this rule is in the case of such famous explorers as David Livingstone, for example, who in addition to his other qualities was also a trained and scientific naturalist.

It would have been easy, in regard to every statement, to allow the text to bristle with footnotes and references. In some chapters there is not a sentence but would have clamoured for these; and the letter press would have been swallowed up by vast masses of comment, like one of those dreadful books we hated so much at school. There is a short bibliography at the end of the volume which will no doubt serve the same purpose, and the more usefully perhaps since the literature devoted to the termite is not yet as unwieldy as that which has gathered around the bee.

So much for the facts. I have unearthed them from all kinds of places: they were confused and vague, obscure, often meaningless in their isolation. As in *The Life of the Bee,* my rôle has been limited to connecting them, grouping them as harmoniously as I could, letting one react upon the other, adding

-C 4 ꝛa pertinent reflection here and there, and, above all, to putting the facts on record, for the mysteries of the termitary are not as familiar as those of the hive to the ever-growing number of naturalists who concern themselves specially with insects.

It is only the interpretation that is more or less my own: it may also be the reader's, for he will perhaps draw entirely different conclusions. Interpretation, indeed, is the one exclusive property of the historian; and the monograph of an insect, especially of such a strange one as this, is after all merely the history of an unknown tribe, of a tribe which at times seems to have been derived from another planet, and a history that calls for the same methodical and disinterested treatment as the history of mankind.

This book may be regarded, if you choose, as a pendant to *The Life of the Bee,* but the colour, the atmosphere, is no longer the same. It is as different, in a sense, as day and night, dawn and dusk, Heaven and Hell. On the one side, if we do not probe too deeply—for the hive also has its drama and tragedy—our first impression is all of light, spring, summer, sunshine, perfume, space, wings, azure, dew and felicity without parallel amongst the joys of this earth. On the other, all is darkness: underground tyranny, cruelty, sordid, filthy avarice, the atmosphere of the convict cell, of the penal settlement and the charnel house; but also, at the summit, a whole-hearted, heroic, deliberate and intelligent sacrifice to an idea or an instinct—the name matters little, the results are the same—a sacrifice that is without limit and almost infinite; and this must be held to compensate for what merely seems beautiful. It brings the victims nearer to ourselves, it makes them almost our brothers; and, from certain points of view, causes these wretched insects, more than the bee or any other living creature on earth, to become the heralds, perhaps the precursors, of our own destiny.

II

Entomologists, in accord with geologists, conjecture that the civilisation of the termite, commonly called the white ant—although it is of a very doubtful white—precedes by a hundred million years the appearance of man on our planet. Such conjectures are difficult to check, and the point is, moreover, as not infrequently happens, one upon which the authorities are by no means agreed. Some, such as N. Holmgren, connecting them with the Protoblattidæ which were extinguished in the Permian, refer these insects back to the boundless, bottomless night of the Primary. Others find them in the Lias of England, Germany and Switzerland—that is to say, in the Secondary; others, again, discover them only in the Upper Eocene—in other words, in the Tertiary. One hundred and fifty species have been identified embedded in fossil amber. Be the truth what it may, the termites certainly go back some million years, and this may satisfy everyone.

Their civilisation, which is the earliest of any, is the most curious, the most complex, the most intelligent, and, in a sense, the most logical and best fitted to the difficulties of existence, which has ever appeared before our own on this globe. From several points of view this civilisation, although fierce, sinister and often repulsive, is superior to that of the bee, of the ant, and even of man himself.

The Life of the White Ant

III

The literature devoted to the termite is far from being as rich as that which has gathered round the bee and the ant. The first entomologist seriously to busy himself with the insects was J. G. Koenig, who lived for a long time in India, at Tranquebar in the State of Madras, where he studied them at his leisure. He died in 1785. Next came Henry Smeathman, who, along with Herman Hagen, is the true father of termitology. His famous *Account of the Termites found in Africa, etc.,* which appeared in 1781, contains a truly inexhaustible treasure of observations and interpretations, on which all who have interested themselves in the insect have drawn; and the works of his successors, notably of G. B. Haviland and T. J. Savage, have in nearly every case established his accuracy. Herman Hagen of Königsberg, in 1855, provided the *Linnea Entomologica* of Berlin with a systematic and complete monograph in which he analysed with the precision, the detail and the conscientiousness which, it must be admitted, Germans bring to work of this kind, everything that had been written about the termites from ancient India and Egypt down to our own day. It contains summaries and criticisms of the hundreds of observations made by every traveller who has studied them in Asia, Africa, America and Australia.

Of more recent works, we must mention above all those of Grassi and Sandias, who determined the micrology of the termite and were the first to suspect the astonishing part played by certain protozoa in the intestine of the insect; Charles Lespès, who describes a little European termite which he calls, perhaps erroneously, *T. Lucifugus;* Fritz Müller; Filippo

Silvestri, who concerns himself with the termite of South America; Y. Sjostedt, whose province is the African termite and whose work is principally classification; W. W. Froggatt, who, along with the naturalist W. Savile-Kent, exhausts pretty well all there is to be said with regard to the Australian termite; E. Hegh, who devoting himself specially to the termites of the Congo, has continued Hagen's work and brought it down to 1922, summarising very completely in a remarkable volume with a wealth of illustrations nearly all that was known at that date concerning our insect. There are also Wasmann, A. Imms and Nils Holmgren, the great Swedish termitologist; K. Escherich, a German entomologist, who has made an exceedingly interesting study of the termites in Erythrea; and, finally, to avoid useless enumeration of all the names to be met in the bibliography, L. R. Cleveland, whose experiments and observations upon the protozoa in the intestine of our Xylophaga, pursued in the magnificent laboratories of Harvard, rank among the most elaborate and thorough in modern biology. Nor should we forget the absorbing monographs of E. Bugnion, which I shall more than once have occasion to quote; for the rest, there is the bibliography at the end of the book.

This literature, although it cannot be compared with that devoted to hymenoptera, is nevertheless sufficient to determine the main lines of a political, economic and social organisation; in other words, of a destiny prefiguring perhaps, at the pace we are proceeding and unless we react before it is too late, the destiny which awaits ourselves. We may find therein some interesting suggestions, some lessons that may be of use. Not excepting the bee and the ant, there is no living creature, I repeat, at the present moment on this earth that is at once so remote from and so near to us, so pitiably, so wonderfully, so fraternally human.

Our Utopians, in their endeavour to describe what society will be in the future, provide bewildering pictures that make our brain reel—and all the time we have under our eyes models as fantastic, as disturbing and—who can tell?—as prophetic as any that could be found in Venus, Jupiter or Mars.

IV

The termite is not hymenopterous, like the bee or the ant. Its scientific classification—no easy matter—does not seem yet to have been established *ne varietur:* but it is generally placed in the order of orthoptera, orthopteroid neuroptera, neuroptera, or pseudoneuroptera, of the division of Corrodentia. As a fact, it belongs to a separate class, the Isoptera. There are some entomologists who, because of its social instincts, would like to rank it amongst the hymenoptera.

The big termite exclusively inhabits hot countries: the tropics or sub-tropical regions. We have already said that, in spite of its name, it is rarely white. It assumes rather, approximately, the colour of the earth it lives in. It varies in size, according to species, from three to ten or twelve millimetres: it is therefore sometimes as big as our small domestic bee. The insect—at any rate as far as the bulk of the population is concerned, for we shall see later that it displays an incredible variety of forms—more or less resembles a badly drawn ant, with an abdomen that is striated crossways, soft and almost larval.

We shall also see that there are few creatures so poorly

equipped by nature for the struggle for life. It has neither
the sting of the bee nor the formidable breastplate of chitin
covering the ant, its most relentless foe. As a rule, it has no
wings; and if, by chance, it is endowed with them, they are
loaned to it merely in mockery to lead it to the slaughter.
Ponderous and devoid of all agility, it cannot escape danger
by flight. Vulnerable as a worm, it falls a defenceless prey to
every kind of bird, reptile and insect that craves for its suc-
culent flesh. It can live only in equatorial regions, and yet—
fatal contradiction—it perishes on exposure to the rays of the
sun. It has an absolute need of moisture, yet is nearly always
compelled to live in countries where for seven or eight months
on end there is never a drop of rain. In a word, Nature has
shown herself, as far as the termite is concerned, almost as un-
just, ill-disposed, ironical and fantastic, as illogical and
treacherous, as towards man. But just as cleverly as man—
and in some cases, at least so far, with even more cunning—
the insect has had the wit to profit by the only advantage a
forgetful, curious or simply indifferent stepmother has had
the grace to leave it: a little unseen power which in its case
we call instinct and, in our own, for no special reason, intellect.
With the aid of this little power, which has not yet even a
definitive name, the termite has been able to transform itself
and to invent weapons that it possesses no more spontaneously
than we possess our own; it has been able to organise, to make
its position impregnable, to maintain in its cities the temperature and the degree of moisture necessary for its existence; to
ensure against the future, to multiply indefinitely and to become little by little the most tenacious, the most deeply rooted,
the most formidable, of all the occupants and conquerors

of this globe.

Such are the reasons that made it seem worth while to interest ourselves for a moment in these insects, at times so odious and at others so admirable—and of all the living creatures known to us the only ones that have succeeded in emerging from a wretchedness as squalid as our own to a civilisation that, from certain points of view, is no whit inferior to the civilisation we are attaining to-day.

II
THE TERMITARY

II

THE TERMITARY

I

THERE are from twelve to fifteen hundred species of termites. The best known are the *T. Bellicosus,* which erect huge hillocks; the *Nemorosus;* the *Lucifugus* which have made an appearance here and there in Europe; the *Incertus;* the *Vulgaris;* the *Coptotermes;* the *Bornensis* and the *Mangensis,* whose soldiers carry syringes; the *Rhinotermes;* the *T. Planus;* the *Tenuis;* the *Malayanus;* the *Viator*—one of the few which sometimes live in the open and cross the jungle, in long files, with soldiers surrounding the carrier workers—the *T. Longipes;* the *Foraminifer;* the *Sulphureus;* the *Gestroi,* whose fierce warriors deliberately attack living trees; the *T. Carbonarius,* whose soldiers in most peculiar fashion produce the mysterious rhythmical hammering noise mentioned later; the *T. Latericus;* the *Lacessitus;* the *Dives;* the *Gilvus;* the *Azarellii;* the *Translucens;* the *Speciosus;* the *Comis;* the *Laticornis;* the *Brevicornis;* the *Fuscipennis;* the *Atripennis;* the *Ovipennis;* the *Regularis;* the *Inanis;* the *Latifrons;* the *Filicornis;* the *Sordidus,* which live in the island of Borneo; the *Laborator* of Malacca; the *Capritermes,* whose jaws, shaped like a goat's horns, act as springs and impel the insect a distance of from twenty to thirty centimetres; the *Termopsis* and the *Calotermes,* which are the most backward; and some hundreds of others that it would be tedious to mention.

One must remember that observation of the habits of this exotic and always invisible insect is recent and incomplete; that many points remain obscure, and the termitary is heavily charged with mystery.

Indeed, not only does the termite inhabit countries where naturalists are infinitely rarer than in Europe, but it is not—or at any rate was not, till the Americans began to take an interest in it—a laboratory insect that, like the ants and bees, can be studied in hives or glass boxes. The great myrmecologists, such as Forel, Charles Janet, Lubbock, Wasmann, Cornetz and others, have not had occasion to devote much attention to it. If the termite finds its way into an entomologist's cabinet, it is as a rule to destroy that cabinet. On the other hand, to remove the contents of a termitary is no easy or pleasant matter. Hatchet-steel breaks against the hard cement of the domes, which have to be blown up with powder. Very often the natives, through fear or superstition, will refuse to assist the explorer who, as Douville relates in his travels to the Congo, is obliged to clothe himself in leather, and to wear a mask, so as to avoid the bites of the thousands of warriors that will immediately surround him and never let go. When at last the termitary is opened, there is only the spectacle of a vast and fearful commotion, and the secrets of its daily life lie unrevealed. Besides, do what one may, one never can reach the inmost subterranean recesses that are hidden several yards below the surface.

It is true that there exists a tribe of European termites, very small and probably degenerate, which were conscientiously studied some seventy years ago by Charles Lespès, a French

Photograph: *Victor Wolfgang von Hagen*

GIANT CARTON NEST OF NASUTITERMES IN THE AMAZON, SOUTH AMERICA

entomologist. They are easily confused with ants, although they are of a slightly ambered, almost diaphanous, white. They are to be found in Sicily, generally in the district of Catania, but most of all in the *landes* in the neighbourhood of Bordeaux, where they inhabit old pine stumps. Unlike their kin in hot countries, they very rarely enter houses, and the damage they do is insignificant. They are no bigger than a small ant, are delicate, miserable-looking, few in number, harmless, and almost without means of defence. They are the poor relations of the species, strayed and enfeebled descendants perhaps of the *Lucifugus* we shall encounter later. At all events, they can give us only an approximate idea of the habits and organisation of the huge tropical republics.

II

Some termites live in tree trunks hollowed in all directions and furrowed with galleries that extend down to the roots. Others, like the *T. Arboreus,* build their nests in the branches, establishing them so firmly that they resist the most violent tornadoes: and the branches have to be sawn through to bring the nests down. But the classic termitary, belonging to the main species, always exists underground. Nothing is more bewildering, more fantastic, than the architecture of these dwellings, an architecture which differs in each country, and in the the same country will vary in accordance with the particular species, with local conditions and available materials; for the genius of the race is inexhaustibly inventive and adapts itself to all circumstances. The most remarkable termitaries are the Australian, of which W. Savile-Kent, in his imposing volume,

The Life of the White Ant

The Naturalist in Australia, gives some astonishing photographs. Sometimes they are plain wrinkled hillocks with a circumference of thirty feet at the base and about three or four yards high, looking like a battered sugar loaf with the top off. At others, they resemble great mounds of mud, or masses of frittering sandstone that shall have been suddenly congealed by an icy blast from Siberia; or a humid chalky pile of gigantic stalagmites grimed with the smoke of torches in famous and oft-visited grottos; or, again, but magnified a hundred thousand times, the shapeless agglomeration of cells in which certain wild and solitary bees store their honey; or mushrooms heaped layer upon layer, tier upon tier; or portentous sponges fantastically strung together; or ricks of storm-tossed hay or corn; or Normandy, Picard or Flanders stooks, for the style of these is as distinct and special as that of the local houses. The most remarkable of such edifices, to be found only in Australia, belong to the Compass, Magnetic or Meridian Termite, so called because its dwellings always face exactly north and south, the broader part to the south, the narrower to the north. Entomologists have hazarded various hypotheses with regard to this curious direction, but have not yet discovered any convincing reason. With their needles, their crest of spires, their flying buttresses, their multiple counter-forts, their overhanging terraces of cement, they recall age-worn cathedrals, the ruined castles of Gustave Doré, or the phantom cities which Victor Hugo fashioned out of a drop of ink or coffee-lees. Others, in rather more reserved style, exhibit a conglomeration of undulating pillars, the top of which cannot be reached by a man on horseback armed with a lance; or rise on occasion to a height of six yards, like skeleton pyramids or obelisks fretted and scarred by centuries more devastating than in the Egypt of the Pharaohs.

The explanation of this bizarre architecture is that the termite does not build its house, as we do, from the outside, but from within. Being blind, it does not see what it is building; it is interested only in the interior of its dwelling; and even if it could see, as it never leaves home it would be unable to appreciate the external appearance. As for the manner in which it thus sets about building *ab intra* and groping in the dark—a method none of our masons would dare to adopt—this is a mystery that has not yet been adequately solved. No human eye has ever watched the building of a termitary; and laboratory observation is difficult, because the termites will immediately spread their cement over the glass or render it opaque by means of a special liquid. We must always remember that the termite is pre-eminently a subterranean insect. It first of all digs into soil, then hollows it out, and the hillock thrown up is merely an accessory though an inevitable superstructure, made up of rubbish transformed into dwellings which rise and extend in accordance with the needs of the colony.

Nevertheless, the observations of a Provençal entomologist, M. E. Bugnion, who for four years made a close study of the termites of Ceylon, give some idea of their method of procedure. The termite in question is the cocoa-tree termite, *Eutermes Ceylonicus,* which has soldiers with a syringe (we shall see later on what this is). "This species," says M. E. Bugnion, "makes its nest in the earth, under the roots of the cocoa-tree, sometimes also at the foot of the kitul palm-tree, which the natives tap for its syrup. Greyish cordons, stretching the length of the tree from the roots to the branches at the top, betray the presence of the insects. These cordons, about as thick as a pencil, are so many small tunnels intended to protect, from attacks by the ants, such of the termites (workers and soldiers) as go foraging to the tree tops.

"Consisting of an agglutination of fragments of wood and beads of earth, the cordons of the *Eutermes* constitute for the naturalist a precious object for study. Having with his knife removed a small section of the tunnel, he is able, with the aid of a magnifying glass, closely to follow the work of reconstruction.

"An experiment of this sort took place in the plantation of Seenigoda on the 19th of December, 1909. It was eight o'clock in the morning and a magnificent day. The thermometer registered 25° C. The cordon facing the east happened to be just in the sun. I made a hole about a centimetre long in the wall, and almost immediately ten or a dozen soldiers appeared at the opening, then advanced a few steps and ranged themselves in a circle, the horns on their foreheads pointing outwards, ready to oppose an eventual enemy. Returning a quarter of an hour later, I found that all the termites had gone back to the gallery and were hard at work repairing the part that had been destroyed. A row of soldiers stood on a level with the opening, their heads projecting outwards and their bodies drawn inside. Briskly brandishing their antennæ, they were chewing the sides of the gap and soaking them with saliva. A piping of moisture, deeper in colour than the rest of the wall, was already visible all round. Soon another mechanic came on to the scene, this time belonging to the workers' caste. First it reconnoitred the place with its antennæ; then abruptly turned about and, presenting its anal extremity, deposited upon the breach a tiny, opaque drop of a brownish yellow, expelled from its rectum. Shortly after, another worker, also coming from within appeared with a grain of sand in its mouth. The grain of sand, serving for rubble, was deposited upon the tiny drop at the place indicated.

"The operation was now repeated in a most methodical fashion. For half an hour I could see, in regular succession, first one worker-termite inspect the breach, turn, deposit its tiny yellow drop; and then another, bearing a grain of sand, place this on the edge. Some carried minute fragments of wood instead of grains of sand. The soldiers, who never ceased to brandish their antennæ, seemed specially appointed to guard the workers and direct their labours. Lined up on a level with the opening, as at the start, they made way as soon as the worker appeared and showed it, apparently, the place in which to deposit its load.

"The work of repair, executed entirely from within, lasted an hour and a half: soldiers and workers (the latter relatively few) appeared by common agreement to share the task."

Dr. K. Escherich, also, has had the opportunity of observing, in a tropical garden, how the *T. Redemanni Wasm.* sets to work; he found that it proceeds on a very different plan. It begins by erecting a sort of scaffolding, in which are the ventilation chimneys, then transforms this scaffolding into a massive building by filling in the empty spaces, and carefully equalises all the walls before completing the edifice.

III

At certain places in Queensland, or Western Australia, principally at Cape York and above all in the neighbourhood of the Albany Pass, these termitaries stretch for close on two kilometres, which are covered, at regular intervals, with symmetrical pyramids—that stand there looking like haystacks in immense fields: or like the tombs in the valley of Josaphat: or like some vast abandoned pottery; and the traveller who beholds them first from the bridge of his ship can scarcely credit that they are actually the work of an insect even smaller than the bee.

Indeed, the disproportion between the work and the worker is almost incredible. An average termitary of about four yards in height would correspond, on the human scale, to a building five or six hundred yards high—such as man has never attempted.

There are similar agglomerations at other spots on the globe, but they tend to disappear before civilisation, as the material, which provides an unrivalled cement, is used in the construction of roads and houses. The termite had learned to defend itself against all animals, but it had not foreseen modern man. In 1835 the explorer Aaran discovered, in the north of Paraguay, a colony with a circumference of four leagues, in which the termitaries were so thickly planted that the intervening spaces were less than fifteen or twenty feet. From a distance they looked like a huge town consisting of innumerable small huts; and gave the countryside, our traveller naïvely remarks, quite a romantic appearance.

But the largest termitaries are found in Central Africa,

Photograph: Victor Wolfgang von Hagen

TERMITE NESTS IN AFRICA (ACANTHOTERMES)

more especially in the Belgian Congo. A height of six yards is by no means uncommon, and there are some that reach seven or eight. At Monpono, a tomb erected upon a termitary that is like a hill commands the surrounding countryside. An avenue of Elizabethville, in Upper Katanga, contains a termitary, cut in sections to let the road through, that is twice as high as the bungalow opposite; and when the railway was built at Sakania it was found necessary to blow up some of these insects' homes with dynamite—and the debris rose above the funnel of the engines. In the same country also are tomb-shaped termitaries, which, when gutted, resemble the real houses with two or three stories in which a man could easily find a lodging.

These buildings are so compact as to remain undamaged by the biggest trees falling on them—not an infrequent occurrence in a country often visited by tornadoes—while heavy cattle can climb to the top, without the edifice suffering, to browse on the grass that is growing there. For the slime, or rather the sort of cement of which the walls are made, having not only benefited by the moisture so carefully maintained within, but being also ground to a fine powder by the insect and passed through its intestine, is marvellously fertile. Sometimes even trees grow upon it and are, strange to say, religiously respected by the termite, that usually destroys everything with which it comes into contact.

How old are these buildings? It is exceedingly difficult to determine their age. At all events, they grow very slowly, and from year to year present but little alteration. They might be hewn out of the hardest stone, so defiant is their resistance to the deluges of tropical rain. Constant and careful repair keeps them in good condition; and as there is no reason short of a catastrophe or an epidemic why a colony that is perpetually renewing itself should ever come to an end, it is possible that some of these hillocks date back to immemorial times. W. W. Froggatt, the entomologist, who has explored a considerable number of termitaries, has found only one derelict, only one over which death had passed. It is true that another naturalist, G. F. Hill, estimates that in Northern Queensland 80 per cent. of the nests of the *Drepanotermes Silvestri* and the *Hamitermes Perplexus* are gradually overrun and at least permanently occupied by ants known as the *Iridomyrmex Sanguineus*. But we shall refer later to the age-long conflict between the ant and the termite.

IV

Let us, with W. W. Froggatt, open one of these buildings that teem with millions of lives, although from without they are as bare as a pyramid of granite and give no sign of life, no indication whatever of the prodigious activity fermenting by day and by night.

As I have already said, it is no easy matter to explore them; and, before Froggatt, very few naturalists had obtained satisfactory results. Improving on the methods of his predecessors and better equipped than they, the distinguished Sydney entomologist first sawed the nest across the middle, then obliquely downwards. His observations, combined with those of T. J. Savage, give us a general and sufficient idea of the economy of the termitary.

In the centre of the city, under a dome of chewed and

granulated wood from which numerous corridors radiate, there is a round mass, some fifteen or thirty centimetres above the base, which, though it varies in thickness with the importance of the termitary, would, if enlarged to human proportions, be more stupendous and loftier than the dome of St. Peter's at Rome. It is composed of thin layers of a rather soft, wooden material, which rolls concentrically like brown paper. English entomologists term this the "nursery"; let us call it the nest, as it corresponds to the hatching combs of our bee. It is generally full of millions of tiny larvæ, no bigger than a pinhead; and the walls are pierced with thousands of very small apertures, in order, no doubt, to provide ventilation. The prevailing temperature is appreciably higher than in the other parts of the termitary, for the termites seem to have realised long before us the advantage of a sort of central heating. Be that as it may, the heat inside the nest is so considerable that Mr. Savage, who one day had opened the great central galleries rather too quickly, declared that there issued forth so hot a vapour that he reeled back, half suffocated, his glasses completely obscured.

How do they maintain this constant temperature, a matter of life and death for the termites, seeing that a fall of sixteen degrees would be enough to kill them? T. J. Savage explains it by the theory of the thermosyphon, the circulation of hot and cold air being assured by hundreds of corridors running all through the dwelling. As for the source of heat—which cannot be entirely solar, as it would necessarily vary with the hour and season—this is probably due to the fermentation of heaps of grass or sodden debris.

It must not be forgotten that the bee also regulates at will the temperature prevailing in the hive and its various divisions. This temperature all through the summer does not exceed 85° F., and in winter never falls below 80°. The thermal constant is kept up by the combustion of foodstuffs and by teams of ventilating bees. In the chamber where the wax is made, the temperature rises as high as 95°, owing to the superalimentation of the wax-workers.

On both sides of this "nursery," from which galleries lead to more elegant apartments, white oblong eggs are piled in little heaps, like grains of sand. Next, as we go down, we come to the chamber which contains the queen. Like the adjacent rooms, it rests upon arches. The floor is perfectly level; and the ceiling, low and curved, resembles the domed glass of a watch. It is impossible for the queen to leave this cell, although the workers and the soldiers who tend and keep her go in and out freely. The queen, according to Smeathman's calculations, is twenty or thirty thousand times as large as the worker. This is apparently true of the more advanced species, in particular the *T. Bellicosus* and the *Natalensis,* for the size of the queen is, as a rule, in direct relation to the importance of the colony. As for the average species, T. J. Savage has observed that in a nest in which the worker weighs ten milligrams, the queen registers twelve thousand. On the other hand, in the undeveloped species—the *Calotermes,* for instance—the queen is scarcely any bigger than the winged insect.

The royal box is, moreover, extensible, and can be widened as the abdomen of the sovereign increases. The king lives with her, but is rarely seen; he is usually panic-stricken, and lurks timidly beneath the huge belly of his spouse. We shall describe later the destinies, the misfortunes and the privileges of

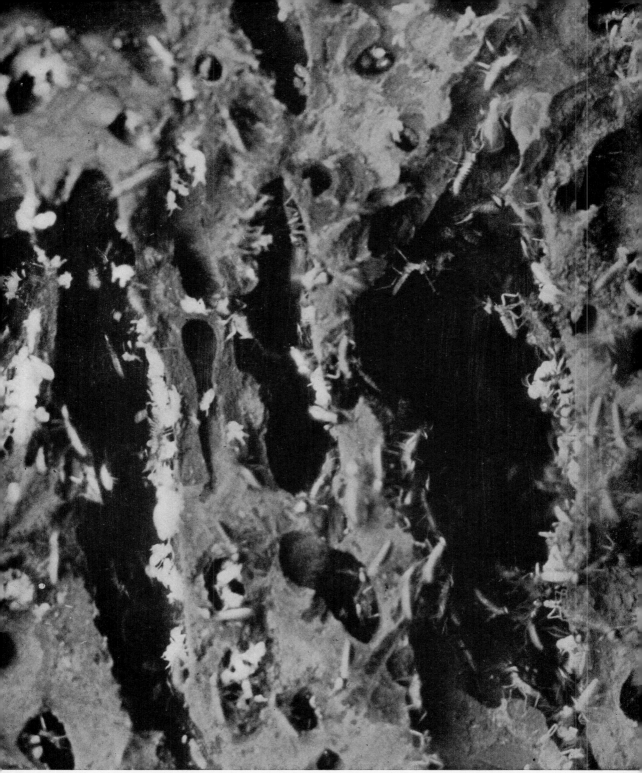

Photograph: Victor Wolfgang von Hagen

THE INTERIOR, HUMID PORTION OF A NEST OF A SOUTH AMERICAN SPECIES OF NASUTITERMES.
THIS IS THE REPRODUCTIVE CHAMBER IN THE CENTER OF THE NEST. . . . THE WHITE MASSES
ARE RECENTLY HATCHED TERMITES STILL WHITE . . . OTHERS, THE BLACK CAPSULED HEADED
INSECTS ARE TERMITE SOLDIERS STANDING GUARD OVER THE YOUNG TERMITES AMID THIS PART
OF THE NEST

this royal pair.

From these enclosures great corridors go down to the basement, where there are enormous halls, supported on pillars. The appointments of these are less known, for to explore them would require demolition with hatchet or pickaxe. All that can be ascertained at present is that there also, as round the boxes, innumerable cells stand one on top of the other, inhabited by larvæ and nymphs at various stages of development. The farther down one goes, the greater is the increase in the number and size of the young termites. There also are stores containing heaps of chewed wood and grass chopped into tiny morsels—food for the colony. Moreover, in case of scarcity, when there is a dearth of fresh wood, the very walls of the building provide, as in fairy-tales, the nourishment required; for they are made of excrement which, in the world now engaging our attention, is eminently eatable.

Amongst certain species, a considerable portion of the upper floors is reserved for the cultivation of special mushrooms which take the place of the protozoa we shall refer to in the next chapter; and, like them, are able to transform the old wood or the dried grass and render them assimilable.

In other colonies, actual cemeteries are found in the upper part of the hillock. It may be conjectured that in the event of an accident or an epidemic, the termites inhabiting such colonies, being unable to keep pace with death and to devour betimes the excessive number of corpses, stack them in heaps close to the surface so that they may be rapidly dried up by the heat of the sun. They then reduce them to powder, and so constitute a reserve of victuals with which to feed the youth of the city.

The *Drepanotermes Silvestri* has even live reserves, running meat as it were; although in this context such an expression is altogether inapt, for the meat in question has ceased to have any means of locomotion. When, for some reason which we cannot divine, the occult government of the termitary has decided that the number of nymphs exceeds the demand, the supernumeraries are penned in separate apartments, after first having their feet clipped so as not to lose their plumpness by useless exercise, and are then devoured in accordance with the needs of the community.

This same *Drepanotermes* has also its own sanitary installations. Droppings are accumulated in corners, where they harden and doubtless become more appetizing.

Such, in their main outlines, are the dispositions of the termitary. They exhibit, however, many variations; for there is no animal, as we shall more than once have occasion to observe, so little bound by routine as our insect, or so ready to display almost human adaptability to circumstance.

V

From the immense vault which, as a rule, penetrates as far below ground as it rises above, innumerable and interminable corridors radiate, stretching far away to distances it has not yet been possible to calculate, till they reach the trees, the brushwood, the grass or the houses, which provide the cellulose. Thus certain regions in Ceylon and Australia, especially Thursday Island and the Cape York Archipelago, are completely mined for miles by the subterranean galleries of these gnomes, and rendered quite uninhabitable.

The Life of the White Ant

In the Transvaal and Natal the ground is furrowed with termitaries from one end of the country to the other: and C. Fuller has discovered there, on two small surfaces of 635 square yards, fourteen and sixteen nests respectively belonging to six different species. In Upper Katanga every couple of acres will often have its termitary six yards high.

In contradistinction to the ant, which circulates freely on the surface of the ground, the termites, with the exception of the winged adults we shall refer to later, never leave the close, damp darkness of their tomb. They never make their way to the open; they are born, they live and they die without seeing the light of day. In a word, there is no insect more secluded. They are doomed to everlasting darkness. If, in order to replenish their larder they have to pass over obstacles through which they cannot pierce their way, the sappers and engineers of the city are pressed into service. These will devise solid galleries made out of a mixture of wood and excrement that have been scientifically chewed up. The galleries are tubular when they have no support; but the artisans avail themselves, with extraordinary skill, of every circumstance that shall permit the least economy of work and raw material. They enlarge, straighten, level; every gap is rounded and polished. If the gallery runs alongside a partition, it will become semi-tubular; if it can follow the angle formed by two walls, it will be merely covered with cement, thereby saving two-thirds of the work. In these corridors, nicely adapted to the size of the insect, sidings are contrived at intervals like those on our narrow mountain paths, so as to allow the carriers, laden with victuals, to pass without difficulty. Sometimes, as Smeathman has observed, when the traffic is dense, they keep one way for going and another for returning.

We must not leave this hypogeum without calling attention to one of the most marvellous and mysterious features of a world already so full of marvels and mysteries. I have referred before to the strange, constant moisture the termites contrive to maintain in their dwellings, despite the aridity of the calcined air and earth, despite the relentless heat of the never-ending tropical summers which dry up the springs, devour every living thing on the earth and wither great trees down to their very roots. The phenomenon is so rare that Dr. David Livingstone, the great explorer and an extremely able naturalist to boot, whom Stanley met in 1871 on the banks of Lake Tanganyika, marvelled whether, by some process as yet unknown to us, the inhabitants of the termitary had not succeeded in combining the oxygen of the atmosphere with the hydrogen of their vegetable food so as to replace, in the degree of its evaporisation, the water they require. The enigma has not yet been solved, but the hypothesis may well be true. We shall have more than one occasion to observe that the termites are chemists and biologists from whom we might have much to learn.

Photograph: Victor Wolfgang von Hagen

THE TUBULAR GALLERIES OF A SPECIES OF *Heterotermes* OF HONDURAS. THE TUBE IS BUILT BY THE WORKERS IN ORDER TO REACH THEIR FEEDING GROUNDS AND PREVENT THEIR BEING EXPOSED TO THE ATTACK OF ANTS. IN THE UNITED STATES A SPECIES OF RETICULITERMES (THE SO-CALLED DAMPWOOD TERMITE) BUILDS THE SAME SORT OF TUBING

Photograph: Victor Wolfgang von Hagen

WORKERS OF THE KALOTERMES, A SPECIES COMMON IN THE UNITED STATES, BORING IN THE CENTER OF A PIECE OF WOOD. NOTE IN LOWER RIGHT HAND CORNER THE CHARACTERISTIC WOOD-PELLETS, DUNG OF THE KALOTERMES

III
THE PROBLEM OF NUTRITION

III

THE PROBLEM OF NUTRITION

I

THEY have notably solved once and for all, and more perfectly and more scientifically than any other animal—with the possible exception of certain kinds of fish—the essential problem of life, namely, the problem of nutrition. They feed exclusively on cellulose which, with the exception of minerals, is the most widely distributed substance on our earth, inasmuch as it constitutes the solid part, the framework, of all growing matter. So wherever there is a wood, roots, branches, grass of any sort, they find inexhaustible reserves. But, in common with most animals, they cannot digest cellulose. How then do they succeed in assimilating it? There are two ways, both equally ingenious, practised by the different species. In the case of the mushroom-cultivating termites (we shall describe them later), the problem presents no great difficulties, but as regards the others, the matter had remained very perplexing; and it is only recently that Mr. L. R. Cleveland has been able, thanks to the powerful resources of his laboratory at Harvard University, to solve it completely. He first ascertained that, of all animals that have been under observation, xylophagous termites possess the most varied and the most numerous intestinal fauna. These constitute very nearly half the weight of the insect. Its entrails are literally crammed with four kinds of flagellated protozoa, these being, in order of their size, the *Trichonympha Campanula,* which swarms in millions, the *Leidyopsis Sphærica,* the *Trichomonas* and the *Streblomastix Strix.* They are found in no other animal. If, to eliminate this fauna, the termite is subjected for twenty-four hours to a temperature of 36° C., the insect apparently suffers no inconvenience itself, but all its abdominal parasites are destroyed. When the termite has been thus liberated, or "defaunated"—to use the technical term—it can survive, if fed on cellulose, from ten to twenty days, and thereafter dies of hunger. But if its protozoa be restored to it before the fatal date, it goes on living indefinitely.[1]

Under the microscope, the protozoan can be seen in the intestine of its host absorbing particles of wood by invagination, digesting them, and then dying, to be digested in turn by the termite.

It may be useful to add that Cleveland's experiments have been made upon more than a hundred thousand termites.

Their method of fixing the atmospheric nitrogen which they require to manufacture their proteins, and of transforming the carbohydrates into proteins, is a problem that has not yet been solved.

[1] According to Cleveland's experiments, *Trichonympha* and *Leidyopsis* both allow their host to live indefinitely, but *Trichomonas,* when alone, does not enable it to live for more than sixty or seventy days. As for *Streblomastix,* it has no influence whatever on the life of its host: its existence, like that of the termite's, depends on the presence of other protozoa. If *Trichonympha* is eliminated, *Leidyopsis* alone multiplies more actively and fills the place of *Trichonympha.* If *Trichonympha* and *Leidyopsis* both disappear, *Trichomonas* partly makes up for their absence.

These interesting experiments were made upon the big Pacific termite: *Termopsis Nevadensis Hagen.* The elimination of any one of the four protozoa can be obtained at will by a course of fasting or a process of oxygenation. For example, after six days' fasting *Trichonympha Campanula* perishes, the other three survive: after eight days *Leidyopsis Sphærica* succumbs: after twenty-four hours' oxygenation, *Trichomonas* dies, whereas the other three hold out, and so forth.

Other species, of considerable size and a more advanced civilisation, have no intestinal protozoa, but entrust the preliminary digestion of the cellulose to tiny cryptogams, the spores of which they sow on a carefully prepared mixture. In this way they lay out, in the centre of the termitary, vast mushroom beds which they cultivate as systematically as do our own specialist growers of the edible Agaric in the ancient quarries near Paris. They are veritable gardens in which stacks arise that are specially reserved for an Agaric (*Volvaria eurhiza*) and a Xylaria (*Xylaria nigripes*). The insect's methods are as yet unknown to us, for every effort to produce in laboratories the white balls of this Agaric, termed mycelia, has failed: they thrive only in the termitary.

When the termites forsake their native city to emigrate or found a new colony, they are careful always to carry with them a certain number of these mushrooms, or at least of their conidia, which are the reproductive cells.

What is the origin of this double digestion? To explain it, we are driven to conjectures of varying degrees of probability. It may be that, millions of years ago, the ancestors of the termite that one discovers in the Secondary or the Tertiary had an abundance of food which they were able immediately to digest without the aid of a parasite. Did a long dearth ensue, compelling them to feed on fragments of wood, and did only those survive which, amongst thousands of other infusoria, harboured the particular protozoa?

The termites of to-day are still able to digest, unaided, the mould which, as we know, consists of vegetable matter in decomposition or already digested by bacteria. Termites that are on the verge of death from hunger, owing to their protozoa having been suppressed, will recover and thrive indefinitely if placed on a strict diet of this vegetable mould. It is true that with such a diet the protozoa quickly reappear in the intestine.

But why have they abandoned the vegetable mould? Is it because in hot countries it is less plentiful, less easy of access, than cellulose properly so called? Is it due to the appearance of the ant, whereby replenishment of the mould was rendered more difficult and more dangerous? Mr. Cleveland conjectures that, whilst feeding on vegetable mould, they were at the same time absorbing particles of wood containing protozoa, which multiplied and accustomed them to exclusive xylophagy.

All these hypotheses are more or less debatable. But there is one that is not taken into account: the intelligence and the will of the termites. Why not recognise that they may themselves have found it more convenient, preferable, to install digestive protozoa in their own bodies, so as to be able to give up vegetable mould and eat whatever they chose? This is undoubtedly what man would have done in their place.

As for the mushroom-cultivating termites, the last hypothesis is the only one that seems plausible. It is evident that at first mushrooms grew spontaneously upon the debris of grass and wood that accumulated in the cellars. The termites must have noticed that such mushrooms provided a far richer, more certain and more directly assimilable food than vegetable mould or waste wood, and possessed the additional advantage of helping them to get rid of the embarrassing protozoa whose weight was becoming so oppressive. Thenceforward they proceeded systematically to cultivate these cryptogams. They brought this cultivation to such a high point of perfection that at the present day, by assiduous weeding, they are able to eliminate all other kinds springing up in their gardens, and tolerate only two varieties, the Agaric and the Xylaria, which are admittedly the best. In addition, side by side with gardens in actual cultivation, they prepare supplementary gardens, spare gardens, with reserves of seed intended for the rapid construction of auxiliary beds to take the place of any which might suddenly become exhausted or turn out barren, as frequently happens in the fantastic world of cryptogams.

Evidently, or at least probably, all this is due merely to chance: as chance also must be responsible for the idea of cultivating mushrooms in stacks, the most practical method, as witness the beds in the neighbourhood of Paris.

Let us not forget, by the way, that most of our own inventions can be attributed to chance. In nearly every case it is a suggestion, a hint from Nature, which sets us on the road. The important thing is to profit by the hint, to develop it and carry it further: and this is precisely what the termites have done, as ingeniously and methodically as we could have ourselves. In the case of man, these things become the triumph of his intellect; what is done by the termites we ascribe to the force of circumstance or Nature's own special genius.

IV
THE WORKERS

IV

THE WORKERS

THE social and economic organisation of the termitary is much more curious, more complicated than that of the hives. In the hive we find the working bees, eggs, males and a queen, the last merely a worker whose reproductive organs have been considerably developed. All this population feeds on the honey and pollen gathered by the workers. In the termitary the variety of types is amazing. According to Fritz Müller, Grassi and Sandias, who are the classics of termitology, from eleven to fifteen different forms can be counted among individuals hatched from eggs that are to all appearance identical. We shall not embark on a complicated and highly technical account of certain of these forms, which for lack of a better description have been called Nos. 1, 2 and 3, but will confine ourselves to a study of these three castes (they include also subdivisions), which we may describe as the working caste, the reproducing caste, and the warriors.

In the hive, as we know, the female rules alone: there is absolute matriarchy. At some prehistoric epoch, revolution or evolution will have relegated males to the background; and now a bare few hundred of them are tolerated for a period, and regarded as a troublesome but inevitable misfortune. Hatched from eggs similar to those from which the workers are born except that they are not impregnated, they form a caste of royal sluggards: gluttonous, roisterous, self-indulgent, licentious, imbecile, veritable encumberers of the earth, and manifest objects of contempt. Their eyes are magnificent, but they have a mere particle of brain and are unprovided with a single weapon; for they lack the sting of the worker bee, which actually is no more than an oviduct transformed by immemorial virginity into a poisoned stiletto. When the nuptial flight is over and their mission has been fulfilled, they are ignominiously slaughtered; for the prudent and pitiless virgins disdain to draw on such miserable rabble the precious, delicate dagger which is reserved for enemies of account. They are content to pluck a wing from the drones and hurl them out of the hive; and very soon they will perish of cold and hunger.

In the termitary voluntary castration takes the place of matriarchy. The workers may be male or female, but their sex is completely atrophied and hardly differentiated. They are stone-blind: they have no weapons, no wings. It is their exclusive task to gather the harvest, to prepare and digest the cellulose; and it is they who feed all the other inhabitants. Apart from them, none of these inhabitants, be it the king, the queen, the warriors or the strange substitutes and winged adults we shall mention later, is able to benefit by the food within their reach. They would all die of starvation, though perched on the most magnificent heap of cellulose: some—the warriors, for instance—because their mandibles are so huge as to preclude access to the mouth; others, such as the king, the queen, the winged adults which leave the nest, and the individuals kept in reserve to fill the place in case of need of sovereigns that have died or are ineffective, because of the lack of protozoa in their intestines. The workers alone are able to eat and to digest. They are, as it were, the collective stomach and belly of the population. When a termite of whatsoever class feels hungry, it taps a passing worker with its antenna. If the suppliant is very young, capable of becoming a king, a queen or a winged termite, the worker immediately gives whatever it may have in its stomach. If the petitioner is an adult, the worker turns tail and generously proffers the contents of its intestine.

Here we have obviously an absolute communism, a communism of the œsophagus and the bowels, a collective coprophagy. In this flourishing and sinister republic no loss is permitted of anything that, from the economic point of view, realises the sordid ideal that nature seems to put before us. If a termite happens to change its skin, the slough is immediately devoured. Should one die—worker, king, queen or warrior— the corpse is forthwith eaten up by the survivors. There is no waste : the clearance is automatic, and always profitable : everything is good, nothing lies about, everything is edible, everything is cellulose, and the excrement is used almost indefinitely over and over again. Moreover, excrement is the raw material, so to speak, of all their activities, including, as we have just seen, nutrition. Their galleries, for instance, are polished and varnished inside with the greatest care; and the varnish employed is exclusively stercoral. If the matter on hand is the making of a pipe, the shoring of a tunnel, the construction of cells or boxes, the building of royal apartments, the repair of a breach, the plugging of a chink through which a thin current of air might penetrate or a ray of light filter—these being calamities to be dreaded above all—it is again to the residue of their digestion that they have recourse. One might say that they are first and foremost transcendental chemists whose learning has triumphed over every prejudice, every aversion; who have attained the serene conviction that nothing in nature is repugnant, that all can be reduced to a few simple bodies, chemically indifferent, clean and pure.

By virtue of the astounding faculty the species possesses of deciding what their bodies are to be and of shaping them in accordance with the tasks to be fulfilled, with needs and circumstances, the workers are divided into two breeds: the large and the small. The former, equipped with more powerful mandibles, the blades of which cross like scissors, travel far, under covered ways, to cut up wood and other hard materials that shall serve for provisions; the latter, more numerous, stay at home and devote themselves to the eggs, the larvæ, the nymphs; to the feeding of the complete insects, of the king and the queen, to the replenishment of stores and to all the cares of the household.

V
THE SOLDIERS

V

THE SOLDIERS

I

AFTER the workers come the warriors, male and female. Their sex also is sacrificed: they, too, are blind and wingless. In their case we detect, in the act, what we are bound to call the intelligence, the instinct, the creative force, the genius, of the species or of nature; unless the reader chooses to give it some other name that may seem preferable to him, and more just.

Normally, as I have already said, there is no creature so disinherited as the termite. It possesses no weapons, offensive or defensive. Its soft belly bursts beneath the pressure of a child's finger. In its obscure, incessant toil it is equipped with one instrument only. Attacked by the most miserable ant, it is conquered in advance. Crawling eyeless from its den, provided with tiny jaws well suited for pulverising wood, but useless before the foe, it has no sooner crossed the threshold than it is lost. And that den—its country, its city, its one possession and its all, its veritable soul, the soul of its multitude, the holy of holies of all its being, more hermetically sealed than a block of stone or an obelisk of granite—it is compelled by certain irresistible ancestral law, at certain moments of the year, to throw wide open. Surrounded by thousands of enemies awaiting this tragical instant when all it possesses, its present and its future, are exposed to massacre, it has succeeded in achieving, how long ago none can tell, what man, no less disinherited, himself only accomplished after æons of anguish and misery. It has improvised weapons against which its normal enemies, the enemies of its kind, cannot prevail. Indeed, there is not a single animal capable of making a breach in the termitary, or of reducing it to subjection; and the ant can secure a foothold only by surprise.

Man alone, the last comer, born of yesterday, man whom the termite did not know, against whom it was not forearmed: man alone can overcome it, with the help of powder, the pick-axe and the saw.

Its own weapons have not been borrowed, like ours, from the external world; it has done better than that, proving itself thereby to be nearer than we to the springs of life; it has created those weapons out of its own body, evolved them from within itself by a kind of concrete materialisation of its heroism, by a miracle of its imagination, of its will-power; or perhaps because of some secret alliance with the soul of this world, some knowledge of mysterious biological laws for which we still are groping. And indeed there can be no doubt that in this case, and in certain others, the termite knows more than we do; and that the will which with us is limited by our consciousness and governs only the mind, with the insect spreads over all the dark region in which function and are fashioned the organs of life.

With a view, therefore, to ensuring the defence of its citadels, it has produced out of eggs in all respects similar to those from which the workers are hatched—for the microscope reveals no perceptible difference—a caste of nightmarish monsters, which recall the most fantastic devilries of Hieronymus Bosch, Breu-

A TERMITE SOLDIER (*Armitermes perarmatus*) OF ECUADOR. THE HEAD IS EYELESS, SHAPED LIKE A RETORT OF SOME MEDIEVAL ALCHEMIST MOUNTED ON A FRAIL BODY. A STICKY LATEX-LIKE SUBSTANCE IS EJECTED OUT OF THE END OF THE ROSTRUM

ghel the elder, or Callot. The chitin-armoured head has been deliriously, portentously developed, and is provided with mandibles that exceed in bulk the rest of the body. The whole insect is practically one buckler of horn, with a pair of lobster-like pincer-clippers worked by powerful muscles; and the pincers, tough as steel, are so heavy, so cumbrous and disproportionate, that the staggering creature is incapable of eating, and has to be mouth-fed by the workers.

Two kinds of soldiers are sometimes found in the same termitary, one large and the other small, although both are equally full-grown. What useful purpose the little soldiers serve has not yet been fully explained, for in case of alarm they take to their heels as promptly as the workers. Their duty seems to be to police the inside of the city. Some species have even three types of warriors.

A family of termites, the *Eutermes*, has still more fantastic soldiers; they are called nasute, nasicornous, proboscidean or syringe termites. They have no mandibles and, where their head should be, is a huge, weird apparatus, as heavy as the rest of their body and exactly similar to the injection-bulbs sold by chemists or rubber-merchants. By means of this bulb, or cervical ampulla, they project on their foes from a distance of two centimetres—at a guess, for they have no eyes—a sticky liquid which paralyses them, and which the ant, the immemorial enemy, dreads even more than the mandibles of the other soldiers.[1] This elaborate weapon, a kind of perambulating artil-

[1] M. Bathelier, director of the Phytopathological Institute at Saigon, having shut some fifty soldiers of the *Eutermes* species in a Petri basin along with six big reddish brown ants, after the lapse of a few minutes found the six ants entangled and unable to move. If one tried to stir, a soldier would immediately direct its beak at the ant, and administer an injection. Yet there was no contact, and the syringe of the *Eutermes* remained on the offensive only for a relatively short time. The more the ants struggled, the more their

lery, is so markedly superior to the other that it enables one of these termites, the *Eutermes Monoceros,* to organise expeditions in the open, notwithstanding its blindness, and to make sorties *en masse* by night in order to collect from the trunks of cocoa-nut trees the lichen of which it is so fond. A curious magnesium photograph, taken by E. Bugnion in Ceylon, shows an army on the march, flowing like a brook for many hours between two rows of smartly lined-up soldiers, who have their syringes turned outwards, so as to frighten the ants away.[1]

Very few of the termites will venture to face the light of day. We know only the *Hodotermes Havilandi* and the *T. Viator* or *Viarum.* It is true that these, exceptionally, have not, like the others, taken a vow of blindness. They have faceted eyes; and, surrounded by soldiers who guard, superintend and direct them, will go foraging in the jungle, marching in files of twelve or fifteen and in strict military formation. From time to time one of the soldiers of the escort will climb a hill and survey the surrounding country; he will give a whistle to which the troops will respond by quickening their pace. It was this whistle which indicated their presence to Smeathman, the first to discover

---

limbs stuck together and adhered the whole length of the body. They were soon completely immobilised, and finally succumbed.

[1] "The census of the army on the march, as shown on enlarged photographs (magnesium flash-lights), gave figures varying from 232 to 623 for a length of 32 centimetres; that is to say, from 806 to 1,917 termites to the metre. If we take a thousand per metre as an average figure, that would give us a total of 300,000 termites for the whole army marching past for five hours at a rate of a metre to the minute. The number of soldiers on guard counted on one of the photographs was 80 on the left and 51 on the right for a length of 55 centimetres, 146 and 96 respectively to a meter, 242 in all.

"One day, when the returning army was being harassed by ants (*Pheidologeton*), I counted along the basement of the hut, over a length of $3\frac{1}{2}$ metres, a row of 281 soldiers opposing the enemy and covering the retreat of the workers laden with lichen. The latter were marching alongside the wall under cover from the attacks" (Dr. E. Bugnion).

We must not forget that all these workers and soldiers are blind, and should ask ourselves what men would do in their place.

them. In this case also, as in the former instance, the march past of the innumerable troops took five or six hours.

The soldiers of the other species never leave the fortress it is their duty to defend. They are kept there by complete blindness. The Genius of the species has devised this practical and radical means of retaining them at their post. Moreover, they are effective only on their battlements and facing the foe. Turn them round, and they are lost: the head and shoulders only are armed and plated while the hindquarters, soft as a worm, are exposed to every bite.

II

The natural, the hereditary enemy, is the ant; it has been an enemy for the past two or three millions of years, for geologically the ant comes later than the termite.[1] It may be said that, but for the ant, the destructive insect engaging our attention would now be master of the southern portion of this globe; though it may also be argued that it was to the necessity of self-protection against the ant that the termite owes its most remarkable qualities, its highly developed intelligence, and the marvellous organisation of its republics. But this is a problem that we need not endeavour to solve.

Returning to the lower species, we encounter, amongst others, the *Archotermopsis* and the *Calotermes*. These do not yet build, but are content to hollow their galleries in tree trunks. They all perform more or less the same kind of labour, and the

---

[1] Man has taken advantage of this deadly enmity: the natives of Madras, for instance, use certain kinds of ants, the *Pheidologeton* especially, to destroy termites in goods warehouses.

castes are scarcely differentiated. To keep the ant from making its way into their nest they merely block up the orifice with droppings mixed with sawdust. But one *Calotermes,* the *Dilatus,* has already evolved a quite special type of soldier, whose head is a sort of enormous bung, which readily takes the place of sawdust in stopping a hole.

So we come to the most civilised species, the great mushroom termites and the syringe *Eutermes,* reconstructing step by step —there are some hundreds—every stage in an evolution, every successive progress in a civilisation, which probably has not even yet reached its zenith. Such an undertaking, barely outlined by E. Bugnion,[1] is for the moment out of the question, for of the twelve or fifteen hundred species presumed to exist, Nils Holmgren, in 1912, had classified only 575, of which 206 were in Africa; and of these there are not more than a hundred or so whose ways are more or less known to us. But from what we do know we may safely affirm that between the different species that have been studied there are as striking variations in character as between the cannibals of Polynesia and the European races that stand at the head of our civilisation.

All night and all day the ant prowls about the stack, looking for an opening. This is the special enemy against which precautions are taken: the slightest crevices are jealously guarded,

---

[1] The following, according to E. Bugnion, are some of the steps in this evolution:—
1st stage: Heaping of sawdust in the outside part of the galleries. Puddings of varying thickness made of sawdust and droppings, for stopping up exits (*Calotermes, Termopsis*).

2nd stage: Agglutination of fragments of wood by means of saliva or the liquid contained in the rectum, so as to build tunnels, safety partitions and nests that are completely sealed. Cardboard manufacture generally. (*Coptotermes, Archinotermes, Eutermes.*)

3rd stage: Art of masonry with a mortar made of beads of earth and saliva. Perfection gradually achieved, from simple incrustations of earth to begin with, to the most elaborate termitaries.

4th stage: Cultivation of mushrooms. Art of the mushroom-growing termites gradually developed to the point of perfection (Termes).

particularly those that serve the air chimneys; for the ventilation of the termitary is assured by a circulation of air with which our most expert hygienists could find no fault.

But whatever the aggressor, the nest is no sooner attacked and a breach made than the enormous head of a defender is seen to emerge and give the alarm by striking the ground with its mandibles. Immediately the troops on guard rush up, followed by the whole garrison; and all proceed to stop the hole with their heads, brandishing at random, blindly, a bush of formidable, terrifying and clattering jaws; or, though they have always to grope their way, hurtling themselves upon the enemy like a pack of bulldogs, biting furiously, carrying off what they have bitten, and never letting go.[1]

III

If the attack is prolonged, the soldiers are seized with fury and emit a shrill piercing sound, repeated at intervals less than the tick of a watch, and audible some yards away. It is answered by a whistle from inside the nest. This kind of war-song or hymn of anger, produced by the knocking of the insect's head against the cement and the rubbing of the base of the skull against the corslet, has its own special rhythm and is kept going from minute to minute.

---

[1] E. Bugnion gives in his book a very curious picture, taken from life, of this intelligent and vigilant defence. He had put a colony of *Eutermes Lacustris* into a box with a glass top. Next day he found the table on which he had put it covered with terrible ants of the species *Pheidologeton diversus*. As the glass fitted badly, he thought his colony was lost. Not at all. Apprised of the danger, the soldiers had stationed themselves upon the table all round the box: a further body of guards, properly lined-up, stood along the groove that held the glass in place. Facing the enemy with their syringes, the gallant little soldiers had kept watch all through the night and not allowed a single ant to pass.

The Life of the White Ant

A certain number of ants sometimes succeed, in spite of the heroic defence, in slipping into the citadel. Then a sacrifice is made. The soldiers hold up the invaders as best they can, while at the back the workers hastily wall up the openings to every passage. The warriors are sacrificed, but the enemy is shut off. So it happens that we may find hillocks in which termite and ant appear to be living together on the best of terms. As a fact, the ants occupy only a portion that has been definitively abandoned to them, and are never able to penetrate into the heart of the place.

In most cases the attack, which very rarely achieves the complete capture of the citadel, ends in the raiding of such portions as have been conquered. Every ant (according to H. Prel, who has witnessed these battles in the Usambara district of what was formerly German East Africa), takes half a dozen prisoners which, mutilated, flounder feebly on the ground: each raider gathers up three or four termites and carries them off: the columns re-form and return to their den.

The army of ants under observation was ten centimetres broad and a metre and a half long. A strident note was heard from them all through the march.

The invasion over, the soldiers remain for some time on the breach, and then return to their posts or go back to the barracks. The workers, who had fled at the first sign of danger, now reappear; this being in accordance with a precise and judicious distribution or division of labour, which exacts heroism from one class and toil from the other. They begin immediately, and with incredible rapidity, to make good the damage, each insect contributing its pellet of excrement. It has been ascertained by Dr. Tragardh that an opening as big as the palm of one's hand

Photograph: Victor Wolfgang von Hagen

WORKERS OF THE TERMITES OF KALOTERMES. APPROXIMATELY ONE HALF INCH LONG

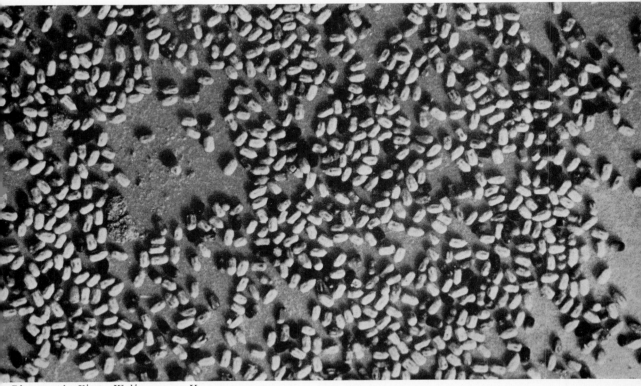

Photograph: Victor Wolfgang von Hagen

THE SIGN OF THE TERMITE: WOOD-PELLET DUNG FROM THE INTESTINES OF THE KALOTERMES

will be closed at the end of an hour; and T. J. Savage relates that, having one evening removed the contents of a termitary, he found everything restored to its place again the next morning and covered over with a fresh coat of cement. This rapidity means all the difference between life and death to them, for the slightest breach offers an invitation to innumerable enemies, and inevitably leads to the end of the colony.

IV

These warriors, who at the first glance seemed to be merely the mercenaries, though the loyal and ever-heroic mercenaries, of a pitiless Carthage, discharge other duties as well. In the species *Eutermes Monoceros,* blind though they be (but every one there is blind), they are sent out to reconnoitre, before the army attacks a cocoa-nut tree. We have just shown how, in the expeditions of the *T. Viator,* they behave like real officers. It is highly probable that the same thing obtains in the cloistered termitaries, although it is scarcely possible to tell, for at the slightest alarm they will rush to the breach, and act as mere soldiers. A flashlight snap-shot taken by W. Savile-Kent in Australia shows two of them apparently keeping guard over a squad of workers that are busily gnawing a plank. The soldiers try to make themselves useful, carry eggs on their mandibles, stand at cross-roads as though directing the traffic; and Smeathman even professes to have seen some giving little affectionate taps to the queen, to help her in the difficult expulsion of a recalcitrant egg.

They seem to have more initiative, to be more intelligent, than the workers; and form, on the whole, a sort of aristocracy in the bosom of the Soviet republic. It is a very wretched aristocracy, however, which, like ours—and here we find another human characteristic—is incapable of providing its own necessaries and depends for its livelihood entirely upon the people. However, in contradistinction to what is taking place, or seems to be taking place, in our own society, the fate of the termite nobility does not depend on the blind caprice of the multitude, but is in the hands of a different power which we have not yet come across, and whose mystery we shall later on endeavour to penetrate.

We shall soon find, in the chapter that deals with the swarm, that in the tragic hours when the city is in danger of death the warriors police the exits, remain calm in the midst of the general frenzy, and act almost as though a committee of public safety had invested them with full powers. But for all the authority which in many cases seems to be absolute, and which the fearful weapons they possess would enable them easily to abuse, they still remain at the mercy of the sovereign and occult power governing the republic. They form, as a rule, one-fifth of the entire population. When they exceed this proportion, when, for instance—as experiments have proved that were made in small termitaries, the only ones in which observations of the kind are possible—supernumeraries are introduced, the unknown power, which must be good at arithmetic, causes almost as many of these to perish as have been imported, not because they are foreigners—having marked them, one can be certain of this—but merely because they are superfluous.

They are not massacred, like the male bees; a hundred workers would be unable to overcome a single one of these monsters, which are vulnerable only in their hindquarters. All that need be done is to stop the mouth-feeding; being unable to eat, they die of hunger.

But what means has the occult power for making its calculations, for singling out and segregating the victims it has condemned? That is one of the myriad questions arising from the termitary to which no answer has yet been found.

We must not close this chapter, that deals with the militia of the dark city, without mentioning some strange, more or less musical, talents that the warriors frequently display. They seem almost to be, if not melomaniacs, at least what the Futurists might describe as the "noisemongers" of the colony. The noises, nearly always rhythmical and responded to by the murmurs of the crowd—alarm-signals, calls for help, a kind of lamentation, various cracklings—incline many entomologists to believe that the termites communicate with one another not only, like the ants, by means of their antennæ, but also through a more or less articulate language. In any event, in contradistinction to the bees and ants which would appear to be stone-deaf, acoustics play a certain part in the republic of these blind creatures, whose hearing is very acute. No sign of this will be apparent when the termitaries are underground or swathed in six feet of masticated wood, as the clay and cement absorb every sound; but if one puts his ear close to a termitary housed in the trunk of a tree, a whole series of sounds will be heard which do not give the impression of being due merely to chance.

Further, it is obvious that so complex and delicate an organisation, in which every element reacts on the other in perfect equipoise, could not subsist without a common consent; unless its miracles are to be attributed to a pre-established harmony, which is much less likely than a mutual understanding. From among the countless proofs of this understanding that are slowly accumulating before us I will draw attention to one only, which is much to the point: there are termitaries in which a single colony occupies several tree trunks, sometimes a considerable distance apart, with only one royal pair. These agglomerations, though disconnected, are subject to the same central administration; and so fully capable of communication with each other that if, in one of the trees, the team of pretenders which the termites always keep in reserve to fill the place, in case of accident, of a dead or not sufficiently fertile queen, should be suppressed, the inhabitants of a neighbouring trunk will immediately start rearing a fresh troop of candidates for the throne. We shall refer later to these substitutional or supplementary forms, which are one of the strangest and most ingenious peculiarities of termite politics.

V

In addition to these different sounds, cracklings and tic-tacs, whistles and cries of alarm, generally rhythmical and denoting some musical sensibility, the termites also execute, on many occasions, equally rhythmical combined movements, for all the world as though they were choreographic experts, or members of some fantastic orchestra. These movements, which have always profoundly puzzled the entomologists who have noticed them, are performed by all the members of the colony, except the newly born. They take the form of a convulsive dance in which, while the ankle remains motionless, the body quivers and trembles, and sways backwards and forwards, with a slight oscillation to the side. This goes on for hours, with short intervals for rest. It will generally precede the nuptial flight; serving, perhaps as some sort of prayer, or sacred ceremony: a prelude to the greatest sacrifice the nation can impose on itself. Fritz Müller imagines that this phenomenon denotes what he calls "love passages." Similar movements are to be seen when the tubes containing specimens under observation are shaken or suddenly exposed to the light; it is not easy to keep them long in the tubes, for the termites bore through nearly all wooden corks or even metal ones, and incomparable chemists that they are, actually succeed in corroding glass.

VI
THE ROYAL PAIR

VI

THE ROYAL PAIR

I

NOW we leave the workers and soldiers (or amazons), and come to the king and queen. This melancholy pair, cabined for life in an oblong cell, bear the entire labour of reproduction. The king—or let us call him the prince-consort—is shabby, undersized, puny, fearful, furtive, and always in hiding underneath the queen. The latter displays the most prodigious abdominal development to be found in the world of insects, a world in which nature is liberal enough with monstrosities. She is merely a gigantic belly, crammed to bursting-point with eggs; a white dumpling from which a tiny head and corslet just manage to peep out, like a black pin stuck in a sausage of bread-crumbs. Sjostedt's life-size reproduction of the queen of the *T. Natalensis* shows her to be one hundred millimetres long with a uniform circumference of seventy-seven millimetres; whereas a worker of the same species is only seven or eight millimetres long and four or five millimetres in circumference.

Her corslet sunk in a vast area of fat, her tiny legs absurdly useless, the queen is absolutely incapable of the slightest movement. She lays on an average an egg a second; that is to say, more than eighty-six thousand in twenty-four hours and thirty millions a year.

If we adopt Escherich's more moderate estimate of 30,000 eggs emitted daily by an adult queen of the *T. Bellicosus,* we get 10,950,000 eggs a year.

So far as our knowledge of her goes, it seems impossible for her, through the four or five years of her life, to stop laying, night or day.

Exceptional circumstances once permitted the distinguished entomologist K. Escherich to penetrate undisturbed into the royal apartment, and violate its secret. He has made a drawing of it which is as haunting as a nightmare of Odilon Redon's or an interplanetary vision of William Blake. Beneath a low, murky dome, vast in comparison with the size of the normal insect, there sprawls, filling it almost entirely, like a whale surrounded by minnows, the enormous flabby inert greasy whitish mass of the appalling idol. Thousands of worshippers are incessantly licking and fondling the monster; but not, it would seem, quite disinterestedly, for the royal exudation appears to be so seductive that the little soldiers forming the bodyguard are hard put to it to prevent zealots from carrying off a morsel of the divine skin to satisfy their passion, or it may be their appetite. Old queens are covered with glorious scars, and look as though they had been patched and repatched.

Around the insatiable mouth hundreds of tiny workers are busily feeding her with the pap it is her privilege to receive; while at the other end another crowd has collected to gather from the oviduct, and wash and carry away, the eggs as they drop out. And in the midst of this turbulent multitude little soldiers are circulating to keep order, whilst ringed round the sanctuary, with their backs to it, formed up in perfect line to face a possible enemy, warriors of lofty stature, their mandibles

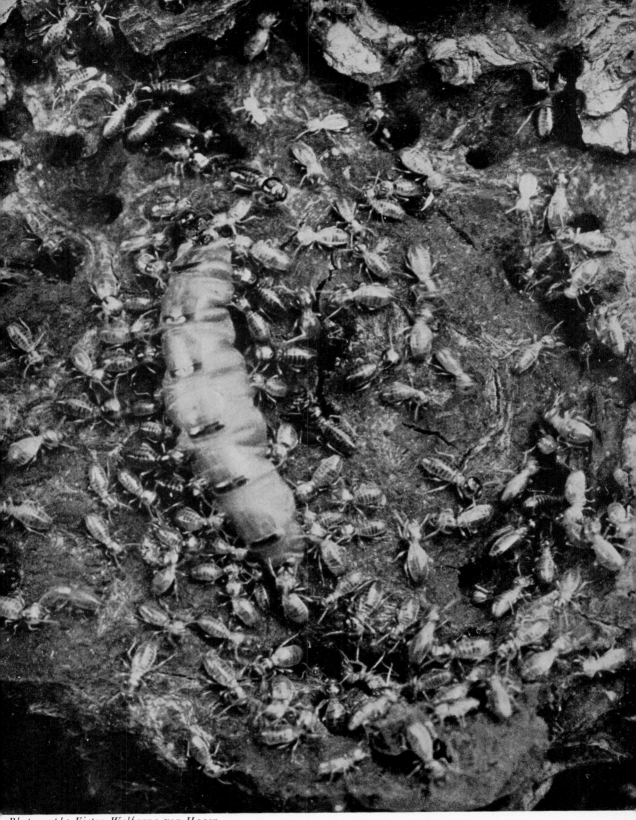

Photograph: *Victor Wolfgang von Hagen*

AN IMMENSE TERMITE QUEEN OF SOUTH AMERICA (*Nasutitermes*) SURROUNDED BY WORKERS

ready, constitute a motionless, menacing guard.

The moment the queen's fecundity dwindles, an order issues—probably from the unknown controllers or counsellors whose ceaseless interference we come across everywhere—and she is deprived of all nourishment. She dies of starvation. It is a sort of passive and very practical regicide for which no one is personally responsible. The remains are devoured with relish, for the queen is excessively fat; and her place is taken by one of the supplementary layers, whom we shall meet before long.

Contrary to the opinion hitherto prevalent, the union is not consummated, as in the case of the bee, during the nuptial flight; for at the time of that flight the sexes are not fit for reproduction. The marriage takes place only after the pair have torn off each other's wings—a strange symbol that would lend itself to much comment—and set up house in the darkness of the termitary which they will never leave till death.

Termitologists are not agreed on the manner in which the consummation takes place. Filippo Silvestri, a high authority, maintains that, owing to the conformation of the organs of the king and queen, copulation is physically impossible, and that the king is content to scatter his seed over the eggs, as they issue from the oviduct. According to Grassi, whose competence is no less, the union takes place in the nest, and is repeated at intervals.

VII
THE SWARMING

VII

THE SWARMING

I

SUCH are the workers, soldiers, the king and queen—these constituting the permanent and essential foundation of the city which, under an iron law more severe than that of Sparta, pursues in obscurity its miserly, sordid and monotonous existence. But side by side with these dismal prisoners who never saw and never will see the light of day, the bleak phalanstery rears, at considerable cost, innumerable legions of youths and maidens, adorned with long transparent wings and provided with faceted eyes, who, in the darkness filled by the multitudes born without sight, prepare to affront the brilliance of the tropical sun. They are the perfect insects, male and female; the only ones with a sex; and from them will issue, if an unkind fate allows, the royal pair that shall assure the future of the new colony. In them are centred the hopes, the dreams of luxury and voluptuous joy, of a sepulchral city, that has no other avenue to the sky or to love. Mouth-fed—for, having no protozoa, they cannot digest the cellulose—they wander idly through corridor and chamber, waiting for the hour of deliverance and felicity. Towards the end of the equatorial summer, with the advent of the rainy season, that hour at last sounds. Then the inviolable citadel whose walls, under pain of death for all the colony, never reveal a crevice other than those necessary for ventilation; whose every channel of connection with the outside world is of stern necessity underground; is seized with a sort of frenzy, and suddenly displays interstices behind which lurk the monstrous heads of the soldiers, denying entrance or exit. These openings communicate with galleries or corridors where all is now impatience for the nuptial flight. Upon a signal—given, like all the others, by the unseen power—the soldiers withdraw from the crevices and clear the way for the quivering betrothal. Thereupon, according to every traveller who has witnessed it, a spectacle is seen in comparison with which the swarming of the bees becomes insignificant. From the huge building, be it stack or pyramid or fortress, often, when there is an agglomeration of cities, from an area of hundreds of acres, there rises, as from an overcharged, bursting cauldron, pouring from every chink, every crevice, a cloud of vapour formed of millions of wings mounting to the blue, in the doubtful and nearly always frustrate search for love. Like all else that is dream and illusion, the splendid vision lasts but a moment; the cloud falls heavily to the ground, bestrewing it with wreckage; the festival is over, love has betrayed its promise and death takes its place.

Aware of the preliminaries, forewarned by an unfailing instinct, every creature that craves for the rich banquet offered each year by the termitary in its sacrifice of the myriads of betrothed—birds, reptiles, cats, dogs, rodents, nearly all insects, especially the ants and dragonflies, hurl themselves upon the vast defenceless prey, the bodies sometimes covering thousands of square yards, and begin the fearful slaughter. Birds in particular will gorge themselves so full that they cannot close their beaks: even man takes his share of the windfall, gathering the victims with a spade, eating them fried or grilled, or else mak-

Photograph: Victor Wolfgang von Hagen

A WINGED TERMITE OF CENTRAL AMERICA (NASUTITERMES) BEING CONDUCTED BY THE WORKERS (THE THICK-BODIED BROAD-HEADED APTEROUS INSECTS) TOWARD THE LIGHT FOR THE SWARM. A TERMITE SOLDIER, THE BLACK-HEADED INSECT (TOP CENTER) CAN BE SEEN WITH THE OTHERS

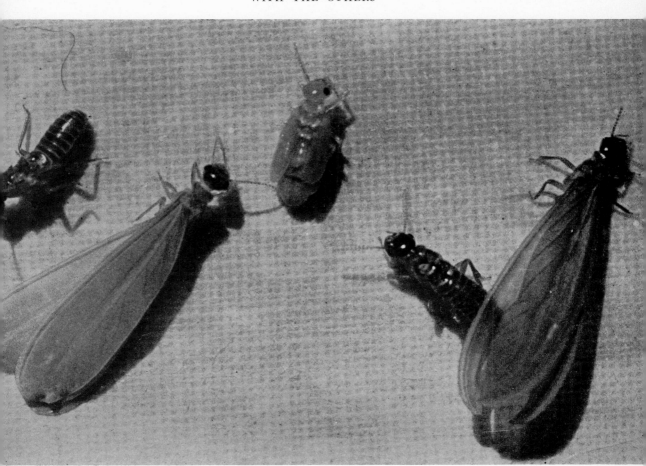

Photograph: Victor Wolfgang von Hagen

THE WINGED SPECIES OF NASUTITERMES OF CENTRAL AMERICA. EXTREME RIGHT, THE GOLDEN-WINGED ADULT INSECT READY TO SWARM; NEXT TO IT, A MALE FERTILE 'KING' WITH WINGS SHAKEN OFF; NEXT (CENTER) A FORM CALLED BRACHYPTEROUS, A SPECIES WITH UNDEVELOPED WINGS THAT DOES NOT LEAVE THE NEST BUT IS USED AS A SUPPLEMENTARY QUEEN; LAST EXTREME LEFT, A WINGED TERMITE WITH WINGS STILL UNPIGMENTED

ing them into pastry which apparently tastes like almond cakes; and in some countries—Java, for instance—offering them for sale in the market-place.

Scarcely has the last of the winged insects taken its flight than —still by the mysterious order of the intangible governing power—the termitary closes, the openings are walled up; and those who have issued forth seem inexorably excluded from their native city.

What becomes of them? Some entomologists declare that, incapable of feeding themselves and dogged by countless successive enemies, they all perish, without exception. Others maintain that here and there a wretched couple succeed in escaping from the disaster, are picked up by the workers and soldiers of a neighbouring colony, and are used to fill the place of a dead or exhausted queen. But how should they be picked up, and by whom? The workers and soldiers do not take the air abroad, or wander on the highways; and neighbouring colonies are walled up like the one that has just been quitted. There are naturalists who assert that a couple can manage to live for a year, and rear soldiers to defend and workers to nourish them afterwards. But how do they subsist in the interval, for it is proved that they very rarely have protozoa and, consequently, cannot digest the cellulose? Evidently all this is still very contradictory and obscure.

II

It is curious that a republic so far-seeing, so tenacious and miserly, should tolerate the extraordinary waste of life, strength and riches that results from the nuptial flight; especially as the cross-fecundation, which is obviously the sole object of this tremendous annual sacrifice to the gods of the species, appears to be almost impossible of achievement. Cross-fecundation can only take place when there is an agglomeration of termitaries —a rather rare occurrence; and all the nuptial flights take place on the same day. So there are a thousand chances to one that a couple, if by some miracle they succeed in regaining their native home, will be blood-relations. But we must not be too arrogant: if such things appear to us illogical or incoherent, it may well be that our observations or interpretations are still inadequate, and that it is we who are in error—unless we are to attribute the blunder to nature which, as Jean de la Fontaine used to say, seems *prima facie* quite capable of having committed a good many more.[1]

Some species, according to Silvestri's observations, swarm only at night or in the rainy season, in order to escape these disasters. Others, to reduce the risk, for several months send out swarms in small detachments. In this connection, it should be once more observed that in the termitary, as in the hive, general rules are not absolutely inflexible. We shall find again and again that the termites, in the same manner as we ourselves and in contradistinction to the habits of all animals reputed to be guided by instinct, are above all opportunists; and although following the main lines of their destiny, are able in case of need to bend them to circumstance as man does, and to adapt

---

[1] With the bee also, swarming is a public disaster and at all times a source of ruin and death to the mother-hive and its colonies, if it should take place twice within the same year. The modern bee-master does his best to prevent it, by destroying the young queens and enlarging the reservoirs of honey; but he is often unsuccessful in arresting what is known as the swarming fever; for he is paying to-day the penalty of age-old barbarous practices of a calamitous, perverse selection, whereby the best hives—that is to say, the hives in which there had been no swarming and therefore a rich store of honey— were systematically sacrificed.

them to the necessity or even the suitability of the moment. In principle, whether it be to satisfy the aspirations of the species or of the future, or in obedience to an inveterate idea of nature, they practise swarming, although it is a prodigious burden and ninety-nine times in a hundred utterly useless; but in case of necessity they curtail and control or even dispense with it, and suffer no great inconvenience from such abstention. In principle, they are monarchists, but, in case of necessity, they keep two queens partitioned off in the same cell, as T. J. Savage has observed; or as many as six royal couples, according to Haviland, not to mention the kings and queens who remain undetected owing to the precautions taken by the workers to assist their escape—these precautions being so effective that Haviland had to search three days for one of the queens before finding her hidden under a lot of debris at the bottom of the nest.

In principle, to complete this enumeration, their queen must have wings and have seen the light of day: in case of necessity, they fill her place with some thirty wingless layers that have never left the nest. In principle, they admit no foreign king: in case of necessity, if the throne is vacant, they eagerly welcome the candidate offered to them. In principle, every termitary is inhabited only by one single well-characterised species: in practice, it has been occasionally noted that two or three, and sometimes as many as five, absolutely different species will co-operate in the same nest. It should be added that such recantations do not seem to be recklessly or carelessly made; a closer inspection always reveals an unvarying reason, which is none other than the salvation or prosperity of the city.

Much uncertainty prevails, however, on all these matters,

and we shall do well, before coming to a conclusion, to await more decisive investigations. The fact that, as we have said, there are fifteen hundred species of termites, adds to the difficulty; and the habits and social organisation of these fifteen hundred species are by no means identical. Some of them would seem, like man himself, to have reached the most critical period of an evolution which dates back millions of years.

III

We have said that the normal régime is monarchy. But the termitary—more prudent than the hive, whose fate depends on the life of a single queen, this being the one defect of an admirable organisation—is more or less independent of the royal pair, so far as its prosperity is concerned. What may be termed the "Constitution," the fundamental law governing there, is infinitely more accommodating, more elastic, more far-seeing, more ingenious, than that of the hive. It denotes undeniable political progress. If the queen-termite, or rather the appointed layer—for that is all she is—discharges her duty generously, she is given no rival. But no sooner has her fecundity diminished, than she is either suppressed, food being denied her, or provided with a number of helpers. This accounts for so many as thirty queens having been found in a single colony; and such a colony may yet be strong and flourishing, not in the least disorganised or menaced with anarchy and ruin, as happens to the hive when queens abound. Owing to the extraordinary plasticity of their organism, which combines all the benefits of a primitive and still unicellular existence with those of a most highly evolved form of life; owing also perhaps—at least we may conjecture this, in the absence of any other explanation—to chemical and biological knowledge yet denied to man, the termites seem able at all times, when necessity calls, in less than six days to transform any larva or nymph, by appropriate feeding and nursing, into a perfect insect with rudimentary eyes and wings; or to hatch from the first egg to hand a worker or soldier, a king or a queen.[1] With this object in view, and in order not to lose time, they always keep a certain number of individuals in reserve that are ready to undergo the last transformations.

For reasons unknown to us, they do not avail themselves of their power to turn one of these eggs—or shall we call them candidates?—into a perfect queen, complete, that is, with wings and faceted eyes, like the thousands that have flown to meet and be impregnated by the king in the royal enclosure. The termites are content, in nearly every instance, to produce blind, wingless layers which discharge all the duties of a queen properly so called, nor does the city suffer thereby. Things happen differently, we know, in the hive, where the worker-bee appointed to lay eggs in place of the dead sovereign will give birth only to ravenous males, and thus in a very few weeks brings destruction and death to the richest and most prosperous colony.

To the human eye there is no appreciable difference between a termitary with an authentic queen and one with only plebeian

[1] Bees, it is well known, enjoy the same faculty in a more restricted degree. By suitable food, by enlarging and more abundantly aerating the cell, they can transform any working larva into a queen in three days; that is to say, evolve an insect thrice as bulky and with considerable differences of shape and essential organs. For example, the jaws of the queen are toothed, whereas those of the workers are smooth as the blade of a knife; her tongue is shorter, her spatula narrower; she lacks the intricate apparatus for secreting wax, she has only four abdominal ganglia, whereas the workers have five; her sting is curved like a scimitar, whereas her subjects' is straight; she has no pollen baskets, etc.

layers. Some termitologists declare that these neotinic layers
cannot produce kings and queens, and that their offspring lack
wings and eyes; in other words, never become perfect insects.
This may be, but so far there is no proof of it; and, in any event,
the matter is of no importance to the colony, whose urgent need
is a mother of workers and soldiers: it can easily dispense with
a cross-fecundation that, as we have seen, depends entirely on
chance. Moreover, everything that concerns these substitutional forms is still a debatable matter, and one of the most
mysterious features of the termitary.

IV

Another subject of controversy, or one that at least has not
yet been sufficiently investigated, is the important question of
parasites (I am not now referring to intestinal parasites), for,
over and above its lawful occupants, the termitary lodges a
considerable number of hangers-on, which have not yet been
examined and numbered like those in the ant-hill. There, as is
well known, these parasites play an interesting part and multiply in fantastic fashion. Wasmann, the great myrmecologist, has
counted twelve hundred and forty-six different kinds in the
ant-hill. There are some that merely look for board and lodging
in the comfortable damp heat of the underground galleries,
and these are charitably entertained, for the ant is much less
bourgeois and miserly than the good La Fontaine supposed;
but a great many others are useful, even indispensable. Of many
the functions are utterly inexplicable, notably the *Antennopho-
rus* carried by the great majority of the *Lasius Mixtus,* that
Charles Janet has so well described. They are a kind of lice,

Photograph: James M. Leonard from a mounted specimen by Victor Wolfgang von Hagen

A GUEST OF THE TERMITES. A GENUS OF DEGENERATED BEETLE (*Termitogaster bicolor*) WHICH LIVES IN THE NESTS OF TERMITES AND EXUDES A WHITISH FLUID FROM THE TIP OF ITS ANUS WHICH THE TERMITES LICK AND LIKE SO WELL THEY HAVE PERENNIALLY ADOPTED THIS BEETLE

and proportionately enormous; for they are as big as an ant's head, which, still proportionately, is nearly twice the size of our own. As a rule, three such lice can be counted on one of these ants, taking up their quarters carefully and methodically, one under the chin, the other two under each side of their host's abdomen, so as not to disturb the balance of its walk. The *Lasius Mixtus* is at first loath to receive them, but, once they have installed themselves, it adopts them and makes no attempt at expulsion. Even the martyrs in our sacred legends would have resented carrying a load like this through life, such a crushing triple burden! Not only does the harsh ant of fable resign itself, but it tends and feeds its charges, as though they were its children. When, for instance, a *Lasius,* bedecked with its monstrous parasites, finds a spoonful of honey, it gorges itself and returns to the nest. Attracted by the sweet smell, other ants draw near and crave their share of the windfall. The generous *Lasius* regurgitates the honey into the mouth of the suppliants, and its parasites intercept, as they fall, a few drops of the precious liquid. Far from objecting, the *Lasius* facilitates the exaction of the toll, and will wait, with its friends, till the satisfied spongers give the signal for departure. Can it be that this promenading of its enormous lice, whose weight would overwhelm us, gives the *Lasius* strange joys beyond our comprehension? After all, we understand very little about the insect world, which is governed by senses and feelings that have hardly anything in common with our own.

But let us leave the ants and go back to our xylophaga. In 1919, according to Professor E. Warren, the number of classified guests in the termitary amounted to 496, of which 348 were coleoptera. Fresh ones are being discovered every day.

There are the genuine guests (*Symphiles*), which are hospitably entertained; others (*Synoeketes*), merely tolerated by careless hosts; (*Synechtres*), which are intruders; and the parasites properly so-called, and unwelcome (*Ectoparasites*). For all the scientific names that are given to these creatures, there is still much to be learned about them, and need for closer study.

VIII

THE DEVASTATIONS

VIII

THE DEVASTATIONS

I

EXPANDING and multiplying in the heart of the tropical landscape, the termitary, with its iron and amazingly ingenious laws, its vitality and terrifying fecundity, would constitute a menace to the human race and very soon cover our planet, had not chance or some strange caprice of nature—which rarely shows so much consideration for us—ordained that the insect should be extremely vulnerable and highly sensitive to the cold. It cannot live in a merely temperate climate, but only, as I have already said, in the hottest regions of the globe. The temperature must be from 20° to 36° C. Below 20° its life ceases; above 36° its protozoa perish, and it dies of starvation. But wherever it can secure a foothold, it makes fearful havoc; as far back as Linnæus: *"Termes Indiæ calamitas summa,"* he said. And Froggatt, who knows them better than anyone, adds: "In the hot and tropical parts of the surface of the earth there is no family of insects whose members wage such an unceasing war against the work of man." Houses are gnawed inside from top to bottom, and crumble to the ground. Furniture, linen, paper, clothes, shoes, provisions, wood, grass —all disappear. Nothing is proof against their ravages, which have something uncanny or supernatural about them, as they are always wrought in secret, and become manifest only at the sudden moment of disaster. Great trees that look most flourishing—for the bark is scrupulously respected—topple down at a touch. At Saint Helena, two policemen were talking under a huge Melia, that was covered with leaves; one of them leaned against the trunk, and the enormous febrifuge, whose inside was reduced to powder, collapsed and buried them in the debris. Sometimes the work of destruction is carried out with lightning rapidity. A farmer in Queensland will leave a cart in a meadow at evening; next morning, all he finds is the iron. A planter will return to his house after five or six days' absence: all is as it was, nothing seems changed, or suggestive of enemy occupation. He sits down on a chair: it collapses. He tries to catch hold of the table: it falls flat on the floor. He leans against the beam in the centre: it comes away, dragging the whole roof down in a cloud of dust. One might imagine some tricksy sprite had been at work, as in a pantomime at the theatre. In one night the creatures ate Smeathman's shirt off his back, while he lay asleep, he had been studying a nest of theirs, and pitched his camp close to it. In a couple of days, not withstanding all the precautions that had been taken, they completely destroyed the beds and carpets of another termitologist, Dr. Heinrich Barth. At Cambridge, in Australia, they raided the grocers' stores, and devoured everything; hams, bacon, macaroni, figs, nuts, soaps: all disappeared. To get at the corks they perforated the wax or tin capsules on the top of the bottles, and the liquids drained way. Tins of preserves were most scientifically attacked: the insects would first of all rasp away the tin layer covering them, then spread a juice over the exposed metal which rusted it, whereupon they bored through without any difficulty. They can pierce lead of any thickness. People try to make trunks, cases and bedding safe by standing them on bottles turned upside down with the neck stuck in the ground, because the insect's tiny legs can get no hold on glass. A few days later, without anyone noticing, the glass has been worn away as though by an emery wheel, and the termites pass tranquilly to and fro over the top and sides of the bottle, for they secrete a liquid which, dissolving the silica contained in the stalks of the grass they feed on, can also tackle glass. Here we have the explanation of the extraordinary solidity of their cement, which is partly vitrified. Sometimes they will do things so fantastic that they might almost be practical jokes. Forbes, an English traveller, relates in his *Oriental Memoirs* that, returning home after spending a few days with a friend, he found every engraving that hung in his rooms completely eaten away, frames and all, not a vestige remaining; but the glass that covered them had been left in its place, and carefully cemented to the wall, so that there should be no fear of its dropping and perhaps making too much noise. There are times also when the practical engineers will make use of this cement to consolidate a beam which has been too deeply bitten into, thus ensuring that it shall not give before the raid is over.

All this work of destruction is accomplished without a living creature being seen. But look closely, and you will find a small clay tube concealed in the angle formed by two walls, or running the length of a cornice or plinth, and communicating with a termitary; this alone reveals the presence and the identity of the enemy; for these insects, which cannot see, have the genius to know what has to be done so that no one shall see them. The work is performed in silence; and at night only a practised ear can detect the sound of millions of jaws devouring the woodwork of a house and preparing its ruin.

In the Congo—at Elizabethville, for example—the inevitable damage they will wreak is taken into account by architects and contractors, who increase the estimates by 40 per cent because of the safeguards that become necessary. Over there, too, railway sleepers are completely gnawed away and have to be renewed every year; and the same with telegraph-poles and the woodwork of bridges. Of any garment left outside only the metal buttons will remain; and a native hut in which a fire is not kept burning cannot withstand the insect's attacks for more than three years.

II

Such are their domestic and normal depredations; but they will sometimes act on a larger scale, and extend their work of destruction to a town and whole countryside. In 1840 *Eutermes Tenuis,* a small termite from Brazil that rears nasicorn or syringe-soldiers, was brought into Jamestown, the capital of Saint Helena, on a captured and dismasted slaver; the insects destroyed a portion of the town, which had to be rebuilt. It looked, writes J. C. Melliss, the accredited historiographer of the island, like a city that had been ravaged by an earthquake.

In 1879 a Spanish warship was destroyed by the *T. Dives,* in the harbour of Ferrol. *The Annals of the French Entomological Society* (2nd series, 1851, vol. ix) quote an article by General Leclerc which states that, in 1809, the French Antilles were unable to defend themselves against the English because the termites had destroyed the magazines and put batteries and munitions out of use. The tale of their misdeeds could be indefinitely prolonged. I have already mentioned that they rendered certain parts of Australia and Ceylon uncultivable; the struggle there has been given up. In the island of Formosa the *Coptotermes Formosus Shikari* even gnaws away the mortar, and brings down walls which have not been cemented.

One would have thought that, the termites being so vulnerable, and fragile, and able to exist only in the darkness of their termitary, the destruction of their domes would suffice to get rid of them. But it would almost seem as though they were able to provide against such unexpected attacks, for it has been noted that in countries where their superstructures are blown up and afterwards systematically levelled by the plough they build no more hillocks, but resign themselves, like the ant, to an entirely subterranean life, thus rendering their capture impossible.

The belt of cold has so far protected Europe; but it is by no means certain that a creature so plastic, so prodigiously capable of transforming itself, will not succeed in becoming acclimatised among us. We have already seen, in the case of the termites of the *landes,* that they have more or less succeeded, in this—at a cost, it is true, of a pitiable degeneracy which renders them more inoffensive than the most inoffensive ant. This may be merely a first stage. At all events, the *Annals of Entomology* of the last century describe at length the invasion of some towns in the lower Charente, more especially Saintes, Saint-Jean-d'Angely, Tonnay-Charente, Ile d'Aix and, above all, La Rochelle, by genuine tropical termites that had come from San Domingo, lurking among vegetable debris in the bottom of the hold. Entire streets were attacked and secretly undermined by pullulating masses of the invisible insects; all La Rochelle was threatened with invasion, and the plague was stopped only by the canal of La Verrière, which connects the harbour and the trenches. Houses collapsed: the Arsenal and the Prefecture had to be shored up; and one day it was found that the archives and all the administrative records had been reduced to spongy pulp. Similar incidents took place at Rochefort.

The author of this work of destruction was one of the smallest termites known to us: the *T. Lucifugus,* three or four millimetres in length.

IX
THE OCCULT POWER

IX

THE OCCULT POWER

I

THE great problem of the hive confronts us again in the termitary, where it becomes even more insoluble for the reason that the organisation is more complex. What is it that governs here? What is it that issues orders, foresees the future, elaborates plans and preserves equilibrium, administers, and condemns to death? Not the sovereigns, those miserable slaves to their duties, dependent for their food on the good will of the workers; the sovereigns are imprisoned in their cages, they alone in the city have not the right to circulate within its precincts. The king is a sorry creature, timid, frightened, always crouching beneath the conjugal abdomen. As for the queen, she is perhaps the most pitiful victim of an organisation in which there are only victims, sacrificed to an unknown god. She is sternly guarded; and when her subjects consider her laying to be no longer adequate, they cut off her supplies; she dies of starvation, they devour the remains—for nothing is allowed to waste—and replace her. For this purpose, as we have seen, they always keep in reserve a certain number of undifferentiated adults; and, thanks to the prodigious polymorphism of the race, can quickly turn one into a reproducing agent.

Nor is it the warriors, unfortunate monsters crushed by

their weapons, cumbered with pincers, devoid of sex, devoid of wings, stone-blind, and unable to eat. It is not the winged adults, who make only one dazzling appearance, as tragic as it is ephemeral: ill-starred princes and princesses martyred for reasons of State, or by its collective cruelty. There remain the workers, who are the stomachs and bellies of the community: they seem to be at once the slaves, and masters, of all. Is it this horde which forms the Soviet of the city? At any rate, those in it who can see, those who have eyes—the king, the queen, the winged adults—are evidently excluded from the Directory. And truly it is strange that, with such a government, the termitary should have endured through the centuries. In our own history republics that are really democratic are in a very few years overwhelmed in defeat or submerged by tyranny; for in matters politic our multitudes affect the dog's habit of preferring unpleasant smells, and will even, with a flair that hardly ever fails, single out the most offensive of them all.

But do the blind members of the termitary act in concert? In their republic silence does not prevail, as in the ant-hill. We cannot tell how they communicate with each other, but must not therefore deny that such communication may exist. At the least attack the alarm spreads like wildfire: defence is organised, urgent repairs are effected with method and system. Further, there is no doubt that these blind citizens regulate as they please the fecundity of the queen; retarding or speeding it by increasing or reducing the salivary secretions which they bestow on her. Also when they consider that there is an excess of soldiers, they restrict the number by ordaining that those whom they regard as useless shall die of starvation and be subsequently devoured. As soon as an egg appears, they decide the fate of the creature to be hatched from it, and, by means of the food they supply, make it, at their choice, either a worker like themselves, a queen, a king, a winged undifferentiated adult or a warrior. But whom or what do they obey: they, the workers? Their sex, their wings and eyes, are sacrificed to the common good; they are charged with all the various tasks, they are the harvesters, navvies, masons, architects, carpenters, gardeners, chemists, nurses, undertakers. It is they who work, and eat, and digest, for everybody; and, groping in their invincible darkness, burrowing in their caverns, eternal prisoners of their hypogeum, they surely would seem least of all fitted to understand, to know, to foresee and distinguish what has imperatively to be done.

Is the explanation to be found in a more or less co-ordinated series of purely instinctive acts? Impelled by the innate idea, do they at first mechanically hatch from the majority of eggs workers like themselves? Do they, then, in obedience to another and no less innate idea, hatch from precisely similar eggs a legion of individuals of both sexes that are equipped with wings, that are not blind or castrated, in order that these may provide a king and queen and shortly afterwards die *en masse?* And does a third idea compel them to produce a certain number of soldiers, and a fourth urge them to reduce the effectives in the garrison, when the garrison requires too much food and becomes a burden? Is this all a mere game of chance? It may be so, although it is legitimate to doubt whether the extraordinary prosperity, the stability, the harmonious understanding, the almost unlimited duration of these vast colonies, can depend solely upon an uninterrupted sequence of lucky chances. If chance can do all that, we shall have to regard it as coming very near the greatest and the wisest of our gods.

But let us pass on, for we are now merely quibbling about words. In any event, the hypothesis of instinct is no more satisfactory than that of intellect. It may even be less so, for we have not the smallest idea of what instinct is, whereas we do, rightly or wrongly, believe that we know something of the nature of intellect.

II

In the case of the bee we note political and economic measures that are equally surprising. I will not recall them here: but let us not forget that in the ant-hill these measures are sometimes even more amazing still. It is common knowledge, for instance, that the *Lasius Flavus,* our little brown ant, has real stables underground in which herds of aphides are kept; these give forth a sugary moisture that the ant goes and milks just as we milk our cows and goats. Others, such as the *Formica sanguinea,* send their warriors out to battle, with the one idea of capturing hordes of slaves. The *Polyergus rufescens* entrusts its serfs with the bringing up of its larvæ; while the *Anergates* have given up working and are fed by captive colonies of *Tetramorium Cespitum.* Then there are the mushroom-growing ants of tropical America, which burrow rectilinear tunnels sometimes more than a hundred yards long; and, by chopping leaves up very small, make a manure on which, by some special secret process of their own, they grow and cultivate a remarkable mushroom that has never been produced elsewhere. Mention should also be made of certain species in

Africa and Australia whose specialised workers never leave
the nest, hang head downwards, and, in the absence of other
receptacles, become living reservoirs, cisterns, honey-pots—
with enormous elastic distended bellies into which the harvest
is poured, to be pumped out when folk are hungry.

And it is as well to add that these things—the list could be
indefinitely prolonged—are not mere idle tittle-tattle, but facts
based on the minutest scientific observation.

III

In *The Life of the Bee* I attributed the occult, provident
government and administration of the community to the "Spirit
of the Hive"—for lack of a better explanation. But this, after
all, is a mere phrase that explains nothing, as beneath it there
hides something very real that we do not know.

Another hypothesis might consider the hive, the ant-hill
and the termitary as a single individual, with its parts scat-
tered abroad; a single living creature, that had not yet become,
or that had ceased to be, combined or consolidated; an entity
whose different organs, composed of thousands of cells, remain always subject to the same central law, although outside
it and apparently individually independent. So in the same
way is our body an association, an agglomeration, a colony of
sixty million million cells: cells which cannot break away
from their nest or kernel, and remain, until the destruction
of that nest or kernel, sedentary and captive. However terrible, however inhuman the organisation of the termitary may
appear, the organisation we carry in ourselves is based on the
same design: the same collective personality, the same unceas-

ing sacrifice of the innumerable parts to the whole, to the common good; the same system of defence, the same cannibalism of the phagocytes in the matter of dead or useless cells; the same blind, obscure, dogged toil to achieve unknown ends; the same ferocity, the same specialised processes of feeding, reproduction, respiration, circulation of the blood, etc.; the same complications, the same solidarity, the same appeals in case of danger, the same equilibrium, the same internal police. Thus it happens that after a profuse hæmorrhage the red corpuscles at once begin to proliferate, in obedience to an order issued one knows not whence; the kidneys help the exhausted liver which has to let the toxins through; and all this without our intellect, which imagines that it governs from the height of our being, having ever been consulted or possessing the power to intervene.

All that we know—and this is a knowledge we have but recently acquired—is that the most important functions of our organs are performed by our endocrinous glands with their internal secretions or hormones, the existence of which was hitherto hardly suspected; and more particularly by the thyroid gland, which checks or restrains the action of the conjunctive cells, by the pituitary gland which regulates the respiration and the temperature, by the pineal gland, the suprarenal glands, the genital gland which distributes energy to our countless millions of cells. But what is it that controls the functions of these glands? Why do they, when the circumstances are absolutely identical, give to some people health and joy of living, to others sickness, suffering, misery and death? It is because intelligence varies in this unconscious region, as in the other; and is the sick man the victim of his

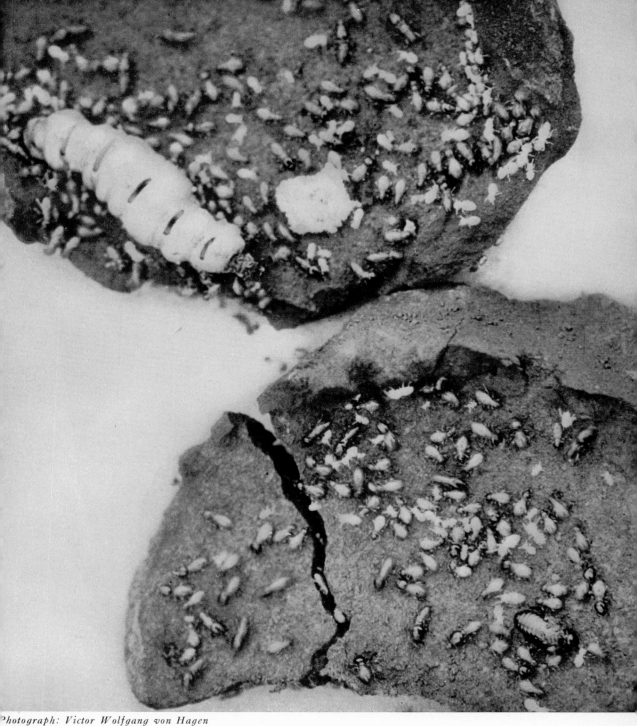

Photograph: Victor Wolfgang von Hagen

A TERMITE QUEEN FROM AFRICA OF THE *Macrotermes* SPECIES. THE LARGE, OBESE INSECT IN THE UPPER LEFT HAND CORNER IS THE QUEEN; THE MASS AROUND HER, THOUSANDS OF FRESHLY-LAID EGGS. THE KING MAY BE SEEN IN LOWER RIGHT HAND CORNER

own unconsciousness? Do we not often find that the body of a man who may have the finest intellect of his time—say a Pascal, for instance—is at the mercy of an unconsciousness or subconsciousness that is inexperienced or manifestly imbecile? Where does the responsibility lie, if the glands go wrong?

We know nothing about all this, we have not the remotest idea what it is in our body that issues the essential orders on which the maintenance of life depends; we know not whether these be merely mechanical, automatic effects, or measures deliberately taken by a kind of central power or general direction that watches over the common good. How be able, therefore, to judge of what takes places away and very far from us—in the hive, the ant-hill or the termitary; how can we divine what it is that governs and administers there, that foresees the future and promulgates the laws? Let us first of all learn to know what takes place in ourselves.

All that we can be certain of for the moment is that our confederation of cells, when it requires food or sleep, movement, heat, cold, multiplication, etc., does what is necessary or orders it to be done; and precisely the same thing happens when the confederation of the termitary requires soldiers, workers, reproducers, etc.

I come back to it: there is perhaps only one solution: to consider the termitary as an individual. "The individual," Dr. Jaworski very properly remarks, "is not constituted by the whole of the parts or by their common origin or by continuity of substance, but merely by the realisation of a function embracing the whole; in other words, by a unity of aim."

We can, if we prefer, attribute the successive phenomena of the termitary, as of our own body, to an intelligence dispersed throughout the Cosmos; to the impersonal mind of the universe; to the genius of nature; to the *Anima Mundi* of certain philosophers; to the "pre-established harmony" of Leibniz, with his confused explanations of final causes which the soul obeys and of efficient causes which the body obeys—reveries of genius, but, after all, with nothing to support them; or we can ascribe them to the vital force, the force of things, the "Will" of Schopenhauer, the "Morphological Plan," the "directing Idea" of Claude Bernard; to Providence, to God, to the first Mover, to the Causeless-Cause-of-all-Causes, or even to blind chance; these answers are one as good as the other, for they all confess more or less frankly that we know nothing, that we understand nothing, and that the origin, the meaning and the end of all the manifestations of life will escape us a long time yet and perhaps for ever.

X
THE MORALITY OF THE TERMITARY

X

THE MORALITY OF THE TERMITARY

I

THE social organisation of the hive is severe enough; but that of the termitary is incomparably harsher and more inexorable. In the hive we find an almost total sacrifice to the gods of the city; but the bee still retains a fragment of independence. Most of its life is spent without, in the radiant sunshine; it knows the happy hours of summer and autumn and spring. Free from all control, it can linger among the flowers. But in the gloomy, stercoraceous republic the sacrifice is absolute, the immurement complete, the supervision unceasing. Blackness prevails: constraint, oppression. Year follows year in unrelieved darkness. All the inhabitants are slaves; and nearly all blind. None but the victims of the great genital frenzy ever climb to the surface of the earth, breathe the pure air, or glimpse the light of day. Everything, from beginning to end, takes place in perpetual gloom. If, as we have seen, necessity demands that provisions shall be sought in places where they abound, the termites travel there through long subterranean or tubular passages, but never work in the open. If it be a matter of gnawing a joist, a rafter or a tree, they tackle it from the inside, taking care always to respect the paint or the bark. Man never suspects anything, never is aware of the thousands of phantoms that are haunting his house, stealthily swarming in the walls and appearing only at the moment of downfall and disaster. In the termitary the gods of communism become insatiable Molochs. The more they are given, the more they require: and they persist in their demands until the individual is annihilated and his misery complete. This appalling tyranny is unexampled amongst mankind; for while with us it at least benefits the few, in the termitary no one profits. The tyranny there is anonymous, immanent, all pervasive: collective and imperceptible. The strangest and most disconcerting feature is that it was not arbitrarily constituted, in its entirety, by some freak of nature: the various stages of its development, every one of which we can trace, prove that its establishment was slow and gradual, and that the species which appear to us the most highly civilised seem also the most enslaved and most pitiable.

By night and by day they exhaust themselves, without ceasing, in various defined and complicated labours. Isolated, vigilant, and more or less useless in the humdrum of daily life, the monstrous soldiers wait resignedly in their gloomy barracks for the hour of danger and self-sacrifice. The discipline is more ferocious than that of the Carmelites or Trappists; and the voluntary submission to laws or regulations proceeding one knows not whence is unparalleled in any human society. A new form of fatality, perhaps the cruelest of all, the social fatality to which we ourselves are drifting, has been added to those we have met already and thought quite enough. There is no rest except in the last sleep of all; illness is not tolerated, and feebleness carries with it its own sentence of death. Communism is pushed to the limits of cannibalism and coprophagy; for excrement is practically the staple diet. To the winged denizens of the apiary, this might stand for a conception of Hell. For one would like to imagine that the bee is unaware of the tragedy of its brief, cruel destiny; that it derives some joy from its visit to the flowers in the dew of the dawn, from its homeward return, drunk with its booty, to the bustling, smiling fragrant atmosphere of its palace of honey and pollen. But the termite—why does it crawl about in its tomb? What recreations are there; what happiness, reward or pleasure, in its humble and lugubrious career? Has it, for these millions of years, been living merely for the sake of living, merely that the race should not die; has it for this reason gone on joylessly multiplying and multiplying, hopelessly perpetuating the most disinherited of all existences, one that is as sinister as it is disastrous?

But these reflections are somewhat naïvely anthropocentric. We only see the exterior, grossly material facts; and know nothing of what really takes place in either hive or termitary. It is excessively probable that both conceal vital, ethereal, electric or psychic mysteries of which we have no conception; for with every day that passes the conviction forces itself more and more strongly on man that of all the creatures in this world he is one of the most limited and incomplete.

II

In any event, if the social life of the termites offers more than one feature that inspires us with disgust and repugnance, it is certain that a great idea exalts them above us: a great instinct, a great automatic or mechanical impulse—or, if you like, a succession of singularly lucky chances—the cause matters little to us who can only behold the effects. I refer to their absolute devotion to the public good, their incredible renouncement of any individual existence or personal advantage or anything that remotely resembles selfishness; to their complete abnegation, their ceaseless self-sacrifice to the safety of the state. In our community they would be regarded as heroes or saints. They practise the three most formidable vows of our severest orders: poverty, obedience, and chastity—here extended to voluntary castration—but has there ever been an ascetic or mystic among us who dreamed of imposing on his disciples the additional penance of everlasting darkness, and who enforced the vow of perpetual blindness by gouging out their eyes?

"The insect," J. H. Fabre, the great entomologist somewhere observes, "has no morality." One can say that, of course. What is morality? Littré defines it as "the sum of the rules which ought to govern the free activity of man." Does not this definition apply, word for word, to the termitary? And the rules governing it, are they not more loftily, and above all more strictly, obeyed there than in the most perfect of human societies? The only quibble one could make would be on the words "free activity," since the activity of the termites is certainly not free. They cannot escape the blind accomplishment of their task; for what would happen to the worker who refused to work or to the soldier who would not fight? He would be at once expelled, and would perish miserably outside, if he was not immediately executed and devoured by his fellow-citizens. Is that not, by the way, a liberty exactly comparable with ours?

Photograph: James M. Leonard

THE ENEMY OF THE TERMITE, THE ANT. SOME ANTS LIKE THIS FEROCIOUS APPEARING ANT *Eciton hamatus,* COME ONLY OCCASIONALLY ACROSS THE TERMITE, OTHERS KEEP UP A RE-LENTLESS PERSECUTION OF THE TERMITE. IT IS TO THIS PERSECUTION THAT THE HABITS OF THE TERMITE MAY BE DIRECTLY TRACED

What does all we have observed in the termitary constitute, if not a morality? Remember the heroic sacrifice of the soldiers who stoutly resisted the ants, while behind them the workers walled up the gates, their sole means of escape from death; thus deliberately handing them over to the relentless foe. Is that not a bigger thing than Thermoplyæ, where at least there still was hope? And what shall we say of the ant which, enclosed in a box and left fasting for several months, spends the very substance of its body, its own fat and thoracic muscles, in feeding its young larvæ? Why should such sacrifices not be regarded as praiseworthy and admirable? Because we conceive them to be mechanical, fatal, blind and unconscious? By what right, by what knowledge? If someone observed us, as obscurely as we observe the termites, what would he think of the morality that governs ourselves? How would he explain the contradictions, the illogicalities of our conduct, the folly of our quarrels, of our amusements and our wars? And how wrong he would go in his interpretations! We may repeat here what old Arkel said thirty-five years ago: "We never see anything but the reverse of destinies, the reverse even of our own."

III

The good luck of the termites consisted in having had to fight a relentless enemy, as intelligent as themselves, but stronger and better armed: the ant. As the ant belongs to the miocene (the middle division of tertiary strata), two or three million years have passed since the termite first met the adversary that was never to cease from attack. It may well be that, if this encounter had not taken place, the termites would have led an obscure, precarious, day-to-day existence, in small, feeble, apathetic colonies. The first contact was naturally disastrous for the wretched larviform insects, and their whole destiny became transformed. They had to renounce the light of the sun; huddled together, they had strenuously to dig themselves in underground, throw up earthworks and walls; they were forced to organise their life in the darkness, to build fortresses, stores; to cultivate subterranean gardens, and ensure their supply of food by a kind of living alchemy; they had to invent shock and missile weapons, to maintain garrisons, to provide for the heating, ventilation and humidity that were indispensable to their existence, to multiply indefinitely so that invincible masses should oppose a solid front to the invader; they had, above all, to yield to compulsion, to learn discipline and self-sacrifice—which are the mothers of all the virtues—in a word, out of a wretchedness without parallel they had to create the marvels that we have seen.

What progress would man have made if, like the termite, he had encountered an opponent on his own scale, one that was as ingenious as himself, as fierce and as thorough: a foe that was worthy? Our adversaries have always been isolated, unconscious; and for these thousands of years the one enemy that really counted has been ourselves. From this enemy we have learned much, three-fourths of all that we know; but he was no stronger than we, he did not come from without, he could bring nothing we had not already. It may be, perhaps, that, for our good, a foe may descend one day from a neighbouring planet, or spring from the very last quarter we should have expected—unless in the meantime we have destroyed one another, which seems infinitely more likely.

XI
THEIR DESTINY

XI

THEIR DESTINY

I

IT is rather disconcerting to note that whenever nature proceeds to endow a seemingly intelligent individual with the social instinct, by organising and stimulating life in common —the starting-point being the family and the relation between mother and child—her object apparently is to subject that individual, as society develops, to a more and more rigorous régime, to an increasingly intolerant and intolerable discipline, duress and despotism. Thus we find her condemning her slaves to a leisureless, unrelieved existence in a factory, barracks or prison; pitilessly exploiting their energy till they become exhausted and die; compelling the sacrifice and misery of the many for the advantage or happiness of none—and all this is order that a kind of universal despair may be continued, renewed and multiplied so long as the world shall last. These cities of insects, that appeared before we did, might almost serve as a caricature of ourselves, as a travesty of the earthly paradise to which most civilised peoples are tending. Our thing at least is certain—the scheme of nature does not include happiness.

For millions of years, the termites have been striving towards an ideal that now seems within their reach. What will occur when it has been completely attained? Will they be happier? Will they at last leave their prison? This seems most unlikely; for their civilisation, that shuns the light of day, buries itself the deeper underground as it becomes more perfect. They used to have wings, they have them no more. They had eyes, which they have surrendered. They had a sex (still possessed by the most backward of them, the *Calotermes,* for instance); they have sacrificed it. And when they arrive at the culminating point of their destiny, there will happen what invariably happens when nature has extracted all she can possibly get from a particular form of life. Another gesture from her—a slight fall of temperature in the equatorial regions—and the entire species will be destroyed, either at one blow or in a very short space of time. The merest fossilised remnants will survive. And all will have to begin again from the very beginning, and all will once more have been vain; unless somewhere things have taken place, results achieved, that we know not of. Not probable, surely: but still it may be.

Even then, this much is certain: no results have reached us. When we think of the eternities that have been, and the innumerable opportunities they must have afforded to nature, there would seem no doubt that civilisations similar to our own, or vastly transcending them, have existed in other worlds and perhaps even on this earth. Did our ancestor, the caveman, profit by them; do we ourselves derive any advantage? Perhaps we do; but the gain, if any, is so slight, buried so deep down in our subconsciousness, that we cannot readily trace it. And even if we could, there would be no sign of progress; but only of retrogression, vain effort and barren loss.

On the other hand, it is permissible to believe that if one of the worlds that swarm in the heavens had attained what we aim at in the thousands of years which have passed, or were attaining it at this moment, we should know. The living creatures inhabiting such a world, unless they were monsters of selfishness (which is not likely, so vast an intellect having to be theirs before they could reach the summit at which we imagine them) would have endeavoured to let us profit by what they had learned; and, with an eternity behind them, would no doubt have succeeded in helping us, in lifting us out of our sordid misery. This is all the more plausible since, having probably transcended matter, they must move in spiritual regions where duration and distance no longer count or offer any obstacle. Is it not reasonable to believe that if there ever had been anything supremely intelligent, supremely good and happy in the universe, the consequences would at the end have made themselves felt from one world to another? And if this has never been done, what ground have we for hoping that it will ever be done?

The finest systems of human morality are all based on the idea that man must struggle and suffer in order to purify, exalt and perfect himself: but not one of these systems endeavours to make clear why it should be necessary to begin indefinitely over and over again. These strivings of ours, that have left no trace behind—what has become of them, through the limitless eternities; in what bottomless abyss do they lie? Why, if the *Anima Mundi* is sovereignly wise, has it ordained these conflicts and sufferings that have never yet had any result, and therefore never will? Why not at once have established all things at the state of perfection to which we believe they tend? Was it because we had to deserve our happiness? But is it fair to attribute greater merit to those who struggle or suffer more than their brethren, when those brethren have been less generously endowed by the external power with the courage or virtue that exalts the others?

Clearly, it is not in the termitary that we shall find the answer to these questions: but it is so much to the good that the termitary should have induced us to ask them.

II

The destiny of the ant, the bee or the termite—creatures that are so small and yet date back almost to the beginning of things—is an admirable epitome, an abstract, of our own, as the centuries have shaped it; and for an instant we are able to hold it in our hand. Let us consider it well. The fate of these insects prefigures our own; has this fate been improved by the millions of years, by the acts of virtue and heroism and self-sacrifice, that would be considered so wonderful if we had performed them? It has acquired a certain stability, become proof against particular dangers; but is it any the happier, can the poor wage be regarded as any sort of requital for the stupendous labour? At all events, it is a fate which remains ceaselessly exposed to the slightest caprice of climate.

Whither do these experiments tend that nature is making? We cannot tell; and nature herself would not seem to know; for if truly there were an object, she would readily have learned how to attain it in the eternity that preceded this moment of ours, inasmuch as the eternity that shall follow will have the same value and the same capacity as that which is past: or rather, the two make one only, an eternal present in which everything which has not been attained never will reach attainment. Whatever be the duration and the amplitude of our movements, that hover motionless between two infinities, we remain always at the same point in space and time.

It is childish to speculate whither things, the worlds, are bound. They are bound nowhere; and they have arrived. In a thousand million centuries the situation will be the same as it is to-day, the same as it was a thousand million centuries ago, the same as it was since a beginning which does not exist, and as it will be at an end which also does not exist. There will be nothing more, nothing less, in the material or spiritual universe. All we shall be able to acquire in any domain, scientific, intellectual or moral, must have inevitably been acquired in a previous eternity: and every fresh acquisition we make will no more improve the future than former acquisitions have improved the present. Be it in the skies, on the earth or in our own minds, only the minutest fragments of the all will no longer be the same; and these fragments will have been replaced by others which will have become similar to those which have changed; and the total will be identical always with that which it is and that which it was.

Why is all not perfect, since all tends to be perfect and has had eternity in which to become so? Can there be some law stronger than all: a law that has never allowed perfection, and therefore never will allow it, in any one of the myriad worlds that surround us? For if a single one of those worlds had attained the goal towards which they strive, it seems impossible that the others should have been unaffected by the results.

One may concede an experiment, an ordeal, that shall serve some purpose; but the fact that our world, after an eternity, has arrived only at where it is, surely proves that the experiments have served none.

If, in the countless millions of planets, each experiment has, without ceasing, to begin over and over again, with nothing happening, does this become the more reasonable because the idea is infinite and incommensurable in space and time? Is an act the less futile because it has no limitation?

What is there to be said against this? Practically nothing, save only that we have not the smallest conception of what takes place in the real; outside, above, below and even inside us. There is the bare possibility that, dating back from a time that had no beginning, on a plane or in regions hopelessly beyond our ken, all things, grow better and none suffer loss. We see no sign of it in this life. But if we consider this question away from our self—for our self confuses the values—all things become possible, become as unlimited as eternity itself; the infinites cancel each other, and therefore fresh chances arise.

III

As a consolation, let us tell ourselves that intellect is the quality that enables us to comprehend at last that all is incomprehensible; and let us consider things from the depth of our human illusion. Such an illusion, after all, is perhaps also in itself a kind of truth. At all events, it is the only truth we are capable of acquiring. For there are always at least two truths —one which is too exalted, too inhuman, too hopeless and counsels only immobility and death; and another which, for all we know it to be less true, encourages us to veil our eyes;

to walk straight ahead, to take an interest in existence, and to live as though the life we have to follow to the end shall lead us elsewhere than to the grave.

From this point of view, it can scarcely be denied that the efforts of nature that we are now considering approximate to a certain ideal. This ideal—with which it is well that we should become acquainted so that we may discard certain hopes of ours that are dangerous or superfluous—is nowhere on this earth so clearly manifest as in the republics of hymenoptera and orthoptera. Leaving beavers out of the question —a race which is almost extinct and that offers scarcely any opportunities for study—the bee, the ant and the termite alone, among all the living creatures we know of, present the spectacle of an intelligent life, of a political and economic organisation which, starting from the rudimentary association of a mother with her children, has by degrees, in the course of an evolution, every stage of which we can follow, reached a vertiginous height, a perfection that, from the practical and strictly utilitarian point of view—and we can judge them from no other—from the point of view of the exploitation of forces and material output, mankind has not yet attained. These insects also reveal to us—whose view of things is personal to ourselves, and no doubt too subjective—a very disquieting aspect of the *Anima Mundi:* and herein lies the real and essential interest of these entomological observations which, without this background, might seem somewhat trivial, vain and almost childish. Let us learn from these insects to mistrust the intentions of the universe towards ourselves. Let us be the more mistrustful since all that science has to teach is, in the main, craftily calculated to draw us nearer to those intentions, which it claims to have discovered. Whatever science has declared has been dictated to it by nature or by the universe: there can be no other voice, there can be nothing else, and this is not very reassuring. We are only too ready to-day to listen to science alone in matters that lie outside its domain.

IV

It is a fundamental axiom of the science of the day that everything, and society most of all, must be subordinated to nature. It is quite natural that one should think this, and say it. In the limitless isolation, in the limitless ignorance in which we feebly struggle, we have no other model, no other guide, no other leader, no other master, than nature; and it is from her also that the occasional impulse arises within us to break away and rebel. What should we do, whither should we go, did we not listen to nature?

So it happened with the termites also. Let us not forget that they preceded us by millions of years. They have an incomparably more ancient past, an incomparably greater experience. In the matter of time we are, from their point of view, the last comers, almost infants in swaddling-clothes. Are we to declare them to be less intelligent than ourselves? The fact that they have no locomotives, no transatlantic liners, no battleships, no artillery, no automobiles, aeroplanes, libraries or electric light, scarcely gives us the right to think that. Their intellectual efforts, like those of the great sages of the East, have taken a different direction—that is all. If they have not, like ourselves, advanced in mechanical methods and the ex-

ploitation of natural forces, the reason is simply that they had
no need to; that, being endowed with a muscular strength two
or three hundred times greater than our own, this strength
sufficed, and required no artificial support or increase. It is
also no less certain that they possess powers and senses of
which we can form no conception, and that these render un-
necessary the multitude of auxiliary appliances indispensable
to ourselves. All our inventions are in effect due to our de-
ficiencies that have to be made good, to our infirmities that
have to be relieved. In a world where all the inhabitants had
good health, where there had never been any sickness, there
would be no trace of the science that, with us, has outstripped
most of the others: the science of medicine and surgery.

V

Again, is the human intellect the only channel through
which the spiritual or psychic forces of the universe can pass,
the only region where they can become manifest? Is it through
our intellect that the greatest, the deepest, the most inexplicable and the least material of these forces become apparent to
us, convinced as we are that this intellect is the crown of our
earth and perhaps of all the worlds? Is not everything that is
essential in our life, is not the very substance of that life, foreign and often hostile to our intellect? And is that intellect
itself any more than a name that we give to one of the spiritual
forces that we least understand?

There are probably as many kinds or forms of intellect as
there are living beings: or let us say existing beings; for those
whom we call dead are as much alive as we; and there is noth-

ing, except our arrogance or our blindness, to prove the superiority of one form over the other. Man, a mere bubble in the void, regards himself as the standard measure of the universe.

Moreover, do we realise how much the termites have invented? We have already marvelled at their gigantic buildings, their economic and social organisation, their division of labour, their castes, their political system that extends from monarchy to the most flexible oligarchy, their commissariat, their chemistry, their transport, their heating, their reconstitution of water, their polymorphism; let us ask ourselves whether, having preceded us by several millions of years, they may not possibly have been subjected to ordeals that may yet await us? May it not have been the subversion of climates in geological ages, at a time when they inhabited northern Europe—for traces of them are to be found in England, Germany and Switzerland—that compelled them to adopt the subterranean existence which by slow degrees induced the atrophy of their eyes, and led to the monstrous blindness of the great majority? Will not a similar ordeal confront us, in a few thousand years, when we shall have to seek refuge in the bowels of the earth to find some last remnant of warmth: and what assurance have we that we shall achieve their ingenious triumph? Do we know how they understand, and communicate with, one another? Do we know by what experiments, what tentative methods, they arrived at the double digestion of cellulose? Do we know what kind of personality it can be, what sort of collective immortality, that demands such unheard-of sacrifices, and at the same time seems to confer benefits inconceivable to us? And, finally, do we know how they have attained the prodigious polymorphism which enables them to create, according to the needs of the community, five or six kinds of individuals so different that they seem not to belong to the same species? Is this not an invention that goes far deeper into the secrets of nature than the invention of the telephone or wireless telegraphy? Is it not a decisive step forward in the mysteries of generation and creation? Where are we in this matter, which is the vital matter *par excellence?* Not only can we not beget at will a male or a female; but until the birth of the child we are completely ignorant what its sex will be; whereas if we knew what those wretched insects know, we could produce, as we wanted them, athletes, heroes, workers, or thinkers who, truly predestined and specialised to the last degree before conception, would be beyond comparison superior to those whom we actually possess. Why should we not succeed one day in enlarging the brain, our specific organ, our sole defence in this world; even as the termites have succeeded in enlarging the mandibles of their soldiers and the ovaries of their queens? This is a problem which should not be insoluble. Have we an idea what a man might achieve, how far he might go, a man who should be only ten times more intelligent than the most intelligent among us: a Pascal or Newton, for instance, with a brain increased tenfold? In a few hours he would arrive at stages in all our sciences towards which we shall doubtless be plodding for hundreds of years; and, these stages once gained, he would begin perhaps to understand why we are alive, why we are on this earth; why so much suffering, so many miseries must be endured before death releases us; why we are wrong in believing that so many painful experiments have been made that served no purpose; why all the endeavours of preceding eternities have resulted only in what we see: a nameless, hopeless distress. These are questions to which, at the moment, no one in the world can give an answer that conveys any meaning.

Such a man would discover, perhaps, as surely as America was discovered, a life on a different plane: the life of which we have the mirage in our blood, the life that all the religions have promised, without being able to offer a beginning of proof. With the puny brain that we have, we feel at times as though we stood on the brink of the great abysses of knowledge. There needs so little to push us in! Who can tell whether humanity, in the centuries of ice and darkness which confront it, may not be indebted to a hypertrophy of the kind for its salvation or, at any rate, for a respite from doom?

But what assurance have we that such a man has never existed in some world of a preceding eternity? A man perhaps not ten times, but a hundred thousand times more intelligent? There are no limits to the extension of bodies: why should there be any to that of the mind? Why should this not be possible; and, if it be possible, is it not reasonable to imagine that it has been; and, having been, is it conceivable that there should be no trace left; and if in fact no trace is left, why hope for anything, or why should that which never has been or never could be, have any chance of ever being?

Again, it is probable that such a man, being a hundred thousand times more intelligent, would perceive the goal to which this world is bound. For us that goal is merely death. But would he be able to see the goal of the universe, which cannot be death; and can such a goal exist inasmuch as it has not been attained?

Well! Such a man would have come very near to being God: and if God Himself has not been able to confer happiness on His creatures, one may well believe that it was impossible; unless the only happiness that can be enjoyed through the eternities be nothingness, or what we call nothingness, which is no more than absolute unconsciousness and ignorance.

What is termed absorption in God—there, doubtless, lies the last secret, the great secret of the great religions, the secret which none of them has confessed for fear of driving man to despair—for man would not understand that to retain his active consciousness to the end of the ends of all the worlds would be the most pitiless of all punishments.

VI

Let us not forget our termites. Let us not be told that this faculty we have spoken of was not found within themselves; that it was given to them, or at least suggested to them, by nature. To begin with, we cannot tell; and besides, does it not amount to the same thing, in the end, and is our own case different? If the genius of nature was able to urge them to such a discovery, may not the reason have been that they threw open channels to nature that we have hitherto kept closed? All our inventions so far have been based upon hints nature gave us; and it is impossible to tell which is man's share, and which the share he derived from the intelligence diffused through the universe.[1]

[1] Let me here recall to the reader what I have already said in *The Great Secret,* that Ernest Knapp, in his *Philosophy of Technique,* has clearly proved that all our inventions, all our machines, are merely organic projections; that is to say, unconscious imitations of models supplied by nature. Our pumps are the pumps of our heart, our connecting-rods are copied from our articulations; our camera is the dark room of our eye, our telegraphic apparatus represents our nervous system; in the X-rays we recognise the organic property of somnambulistic lucidity, the capacity of seeing through objects, of reading, for instance, the contents of a sealed letter enclosed in a triple metal box. In wireless telegraphy we are following the hints given us by telepathy; that is to say, direct communication of a thought by spiritual waves analogous to the Hertzian waves; and in the phenomena of levitation and the moving of objects without our touching them (of which concrete proof still is lacking), another hint is to be found by which we have not yet been able to profit. It would put within our reach a means whereby we shall be able some day perhaps to overcome the terrible laws of gravitation which rivet us to this earth; for it seems highly probable that these laws, instead of being, as was hitherto believed, for ever incomprehensible and inscrutable, are above all magnetic; that is to say, manageable and capable of being turned to account.

XII

INSTINCT AND INTELLIGENCE

XII

INSTINCT AND INTELLIGENCE

I

THESE considerations bring us back to the insoluble problem of instinct and intelligence. J. H. Fabre, who spent his life studying the question, does not admit intelligence in insects. He has proved by apparently convincing experiments that the most ingenious, the most industrious, the most admirably provident insect, if disturbed in its routine, continues to behave mechanically, and to work uselessly and stupidly in the void. "Instinct," he concludes, "is omniscient in the unchanging paths that have been laid down for it: away from these paths, it knows nothing. Sublime inspirations of science, astounding inconsequences of stupidity, are alike its portion; the animal will display the first when conditions are normal, and the second when they are governed by accident."

The Sphex wasp of Languedoc, for instance, is a marvellous surgeon, gifted with an infallible knowledge of anatomy. By stylet thrusts in the thoracic ganglia and pressure upon the cervical ganglia it completely paralyses, without ever causing death, the ephippigera of the vine. It then lays an egg on the breast of its victim, which it imprisons at the bottom of a hole that it has carefully sealed. The larva hatched from this egg will find, therefore, at birth, an abundant supply of game that is alive and always fresh, but incapable of movement or attack.

Now if at the moment the insect begins to close up its hole you take away the ephippigera, the Sphex, having remained on the watch during this violation of its domicile, returns to its dwelling as soon as the danger is over, carefully inspects the cell as usual, plainly sees that the ephippigera and the egg are no longer there, but none the less resumes its labour at the point where it left off, and punctiliously closes the hole which no longer contains anything.

The prickly Ammophila and the Chalicodome furnish analogous examples. The case of the Chalicodome or mason-bee, more especially, is striking and to the point. It stores honey in a cell, lays an egg and encloses it. If you make a hole in the wall while the insect is absent, but during the period devoted to mason-work, it will, on its return, immediately repair the damage. But if, when the mason-work is finished and the storing begun, you again make a hole in the cell, the bee will pay not the smallest attention, and will continue to disgorge its honey into the perforated receptacle although the honey flows out as fast as it is poured in; then, when the bee considers that it has introduced the amount that is normally sufficient, it will lay its egg, which flows away with the rest through the same opening; and finally, satisfied with its work, it will gravely and scrupulously close the empty cell.

From such experiments and many others that it would take too long to recall here, Fabre very judiciously concludes that "the insect is able to cope with accidents, provided that the new occurrence is not outside the scope of what is engaging its immediate attention." If the accident happens to be of a different kind, the insect declines to take any notice and appears to lose its head; it will behave as though it were a mere piece of clockwork that had been carefully wound up, as though every action were predestined; and will blindly and foolishly go on with its absurd routine, until it comes to the end of the series of prescribed movements from which it cannot escape.

Let us admit these facts, which seem to be incontrovertible, and let us reflect that they rather curiously reproduce what takes place in our own body, in our own unconscious organic life. We find in ourselves the same alternating examples of intelligence and stupidity. Modern medicine, with its studies of internal secretions, toxins, anti-bodies, anaphylaxis, etc., could provide us with a long list; but what our fathers, who were not so learned, more simply called fever, sums up in a word most of these examples. Fever, as even children are now aware, is merely a reaction, a defence which our organism sets up by a combination of many ingenious and intricate measures. Before we had devised a means of reducing or controlling its excesses, it usually carried off the patient more inevitably than the evil it was endeavouring to combat. Moreover, there seems reason to believe that cancer, the most cruel, the most incurable of our diseases, with its budding formation of disordered cells, is merely another instance of the blind inopportune zeal shown by the elements that are entrusted with the defence of our life.

But let us return to our Sphex and our Chalicodomes; and let us first of all note that these are isolated insects whose existence, on the whole, is simple enough and follows a straight line that nothing, as a rule, cuts across or divides. The case is not the same with social insects whose life at all points touches the life of thousands of others. Here the unforeseen is constantly occurring; and adherence to a rigid routine would result in never-ending and disastrous conflicts. There is call, therefore, for a certain suppleness, a perpetual accommodation to circumstances that change every moment; and here, as in ourselves, it at once becomes very difficult to discover the wavering line of demarcation between instinct and intelligence. The discovery is the more difficult because both faculties have apparently the same origin, spring from the same source and are of the same nature. The only difference is that one of them can sometimes halt, fall back on itself and consciously grasp a situation, whereas the other perseveres doggedly on its blind and fatal path.

II

These questions are still very obscure, and the strictest investigations often prove contradictory. Thus we find the bees marvellously ready to depart from their venerable routine. They were, for instance, quick to appreciate the advantage to be derived from the mechanically goffered wax frames provided by man. These frames, in which the cells are merely roughly indicated, completely revolutionise their methods of working, and enable them to build in a few days what normally required several weeks of bitterly strenuous toil and a prodigious expenditure of honey. We notice also that, transported to Australia or California, they realise in the second or third year over there that summer is everlasting, that flowers never fail; and they will live from day to day, satisfied to collect the honey and the pollen necessary for daily consumption. Inherited experience yields to fresh and careful observation:

they will cease to make any provision for the winter; and similarly in the Barbados, where the refineries provide them all the year round with an abundance of sugar, they will completely abandon their visits to the flowers.

On the other hand, is there any one of us who has watched ants at work and has not been struck by the imbecile incoherence of their combined efforts? A dozen of them, some pulling one way, some another, start removing a prey which two of them, if they only agreed, could easily carry to their nest. The harvester ant (*Messor barbarus*), according to the observations of the myrmecologists V. Cornetz and Ducellier, offers examples of an incoherence and stupidity still more precise and more pertinent. While a number of workers are busily engaged on an ear of corn, cutting away at the base the husks that enclose the grain, a big worker can be seen clipping the stalk itself just below the ear, without a suspicion that its tiresome and strenuous labours are wholly and completely wasted.

These harvesters, too, will store in their nest much more grain than they require. This grain germinates in the rainy season; and the tufts of corn which spring up reveal the situation of the ant-hill to the farmers, who proceed at once to destroy it. Century after century the same fatal phenomenon has been repeated, but the *Messor barbarus* has learned nothing, and experience has brought about no change in its methods.

The *Myrmecocystus cataglyphys bicolor,* another North African ant, stands very high on its legs and is therefore able to go out in the sun and defy the scorching rays—a heat of 40° C.—which would mean death to insects with less length of leg. It hurls itself madly along, attaining the vertiginous speed of twelve yards to the minute (everything is relative), going so fast that its eyes, which have only a range of five or six centimetres, cannot see what lies in their track. It will pass over lumps of sugar, to which it is specially partial, without perceiving them; and will return home from its long and frenzied expeditions bringing nothing back. Millions of ants of this species have for millions of years started afresh every summer on the same heroic and ludicrous explorations, nor has it yet dawned upon them that their toil is in vain.

Is it possible that the ant is less intelligent than the bee? From what we know in other directions such a statement would scarcely seem justified. Perhaps we are wrong in attributing to the reasoning powers of our bee what may be only reflex actions; perhaps we possess only an imperfect knowledge of the ant; and there is also the possibility that our interpretations are no more than mere phantasms of our brain. Can it be that the *Anima Mundi* makes mistakes more frequently than we have dared to believe? Is this the cause of the insects' blunders? Of our own? One of the most baffling enigmas of nature is the apparent errors, the seemingly irrational acts, that we so frequently meet with. The conviction is forced on us that nature has genius, but lacks common sense; and is not always intelligent. But what right have we, from the pinnacle of our little brain, which is merely a dropping of that same nature, to declare that its acts are irrational? The rationale of nature, if we ever discover it, as we may some day, will probably overwhelm our tiny reason. We are apt to judge all things from the high horse of our logic, as though it were certain that no other logic could exist—a logic perhaps diametrically opposed to the one which is our sole guide. But that is by no means certain; and, in the vast fields of the infinite, this idea of ours may well be the merest error in optics. Nature may more than once have made a mistake: but before we shout this too loud let us remember that we are still living in an ignorance and darkness whose completeness we shall only be able to appreciate in another world.

III

To return to our insects, let us not fail to note that the ant-hill lends itself less readily to study than the hive; and that the termitary, where complete darkness prevails, offers still more difficulties. The question engaging us is none the less more important than it appears: for if we knew more about the instinct of the insects, about the limitations of this instinct and its relations with the intellect and with the *Anima Mundi,* we should perhaps gain some knowledge, the data being identical, of the instinct of our own organs, wherein probably lie concealed almost all the secrets of life and death.

We shall not examine here the various hypotheses put forward in this matter of instinct. Great experts explain it by technical phrases, which, closely examined, reveal nothing at all. Some call it "unconscious impulses, instinctive automatisms": others "innate psychic dispositions, resulting from a long period of adaptation and attached to the cells of the brain, engraved on the nervous substance as upon a kind of memory; these dispositions that we term instinct have probably been transmitted from generation to generation, according to the laws of heredity, as happens generally with vital dynamisms." The clearest and most rational thinkers suggest "hereditary habit, reasoning become automatic." But I could quote others who, like Richard Semon, a German philosopher, explain everything by "engrammata upon the individual mneme; comprising also their ekphories."

Nearly all the experts admit—being scarcely able to do otherwise—that most instincts owe their origin to a reasoned and conscious action; but why do they persist in declaring all the actions that follow this first reasoned one to be automatic? If they grant reason in one case, why not in others?—it is all or nothing.

I shall not allow Bergson's hypothesis to detain me long. His argument that instinct is a mere continuation of the work by which life organises nature is either a manifest truth or tautology, for life and nature are, in their essence, different names for the same unknown; but none the less this too-evident truth, in the development given to it by the author of *Matter and Memory* and *Creative Evolution,* is often very attractive.

IV

However, in the absence of a better explanation, may one not provisionally connect the instinct of insects—more especially that of ants, bees and termites—with the collective soul; and, consequently, with the sort of immortality, or rather indefinite collective duration, which the insects possess? The population of the hive, the ant-hill and the termitary, as I have already stated, seems to be one individual, one single living creature, whose organs, composed of innumerable cells,

are disseminated only in appearance, but remain always subject to the same energy or vital personality, the same central
law. By virtue of this collective immortality, the decease of
hundreds—nay, of thousands—of termites that are immediately succeeded by others does not affect or touch the central
being; just as in our own body, the extinction of thousands
of cells whose places are immediately taken by others does
not affect, does not touch, the life or our ego. Let us imagine a
man who should never have died: so it is with the termites;
for these millions of years the same insect has gone on living,
with the result that not a single one of its experiences has been
lost. There has been no interruption of its existence, or disappearance of its memories; an individual memory has remained, and this has never ceased to function or to centralise
every acquisition of the collective soul. Here we have the explanation of one mystery among many: it leads us to understand why the queen bees, for instance, which for thousands of
years have done nothing but lay eggs, have never worked,
never visited a flower, gathered pollen or sucked nectar, can
yet give birth to workers which emerge from the cell with all
the knowledge their mothers have lost since prehistoric days;
workers which, from the moment of their first flight, know
every secret of orientation, of gathering booty, of rearing
nymphs, as also of the intricate chemistry of the hive. They
know everything because the organism of which they form a
part, of which they are but a cell, knows all that is necessary
to know for self-maintenance. They seem to scatter widely in
space; but however far they may travel, they always remain
connected with the central unity to which they have never
ceased to belong. They bathe in the same vital fluid as the

cells of our own being; but in their case this fluid would seem to be much more diffuse, more elastic, more subtle, more psychical or more ethereal than that of our body. And this central unity is no doubt bound up with the universal soul of the bee, and probably with what is actually *the* universal soul.

It is more or less certain that we were formerly much nearer than we are to-day to this universal soul, with which our sub-consciousness still remains in touch. Our intellect has divided us from it, divides us more and more every day. Can it be that our progress means isolation? May not that have been our specific mistake? Here we have a natural contradiction of our suggestion that great benefit might arise from enlargement of our brain; but, in these regions, as nothing is certain, hypotheses are necessarily in conflict: and again, it sometimes happens that when a regrettable error is pushed to extremes, it turns into a valuable truth: even as a truth that has long been regarded becomes confused, strips off its disguise and reveals itself as merely an error or falsehood.

V

Is what the termites present to us a model of social organisation, a picture of the future, a sort of "anticipation"? Is this the goal to which we ourselves are tending? Let us not say that it is impossible, that our own end shall be different. We arrive much more readily and more quickly than we imagine at a condition of things that we have not dared to contemplate. Often the merest trifle is sufficient to change all morality, the whole destiny of a long series of generations. Did not the immense renovation brought about by Christianity hang on a thread? We have glimpses of, we desire, a life of a higher kind, a more intelligent life, a life of beauty, of comfort, of leisure, of peace and of happiness. Twice or thrice in the course of centuries—at Athens perhaps, in India, perhaps at certain moments in Christianity—we came, if not to perfect attainment, at least very near. But it is by no means certain that this is the direction that humanity is actually, inevitably taking. One may as reasonably foretell that it will follow a road that is diametrically opposite. If some god to-day were to toss with other eternal gods for the probabilities of our destiny, on which side would the most far-seeing place their stake? "Reason," Pascal would say, "defends neither one nor the other."

Obviously it is only in a life that is entirely spiritual that we can find complete and lasting happiness this side or beyond the grave; for all that relates to matter is essentially precarious, changeful and perishable. Is such a life possible? In theory, yes: but in fact, all that we see around us is only matter, all that we perceive is only matter—and what hope is there that our brain, which itself only is matter, can understand anything other than matter? It attempts to, it does its best; but in fact, once it leaves matter, it turns and twists in the void.

How tragic is man's situation! All religions have felt, all religions have agreed, that his chief, perhaps his only, enemy —call it evil or sin, the cause is always the same—is matter; and, on the other hand, within him there only is matter, even the quality that despises matter, that condemns it and would fain stamp it out at all costs. And not only within him, but in all; for energy, even life, is doubtless merely a form, a movement, of matter; and matter itself, as we view it in its vastest form, where it appears to us for ever dead, inert and motionless—matter itself, by some supreme contradiction, is animated by an existence incomparably more spiritual than that of our mind. Is it not from the most mysterious, the most intangible and imponderable of forces that it derives the elastic, ethereal fluid that confers the fearful, vertiginous, untiring, immortal life of its electrons, which since the beginning of things have been whirling like frantic planets around a central nucleus?

But take whatever direction we may, we shall arrive somewhere, attain something: and that something will be other than annihilation, for of all the incomprehensible problems which distract this thin brain of ours, annihilation is surely the most incomprehensible. It is true that annihilation, to us, means the loss of our identity, of the little memories of our ego—in other words, unconsciousness. But that implies too narrow a vision.

There must be one of two things: either our ego will become so great, so universal, that it will lose or completely shake off the memory of the absurd little animal it was on this earth, or else it will go on being small, and will drag this wretched image through the countless eternities: a malediction beyond the torments of the Christian Hell.

Arrived wherever it may be, and conscious or unconscious, we shall adapt ourselves to whatever we may find there, until such time as our race comes to an end. And when our race has perished, another will start a new cycle; and so on indefinitely, for let us not forget that the myth that applies to us is not Prometheus, but Sisyphus or the Danaïds. In any event let us tell ourselves, till certitude comes, that the ideal of the soul of this world does not altogether conform with the ideal, in conflict with all that we see around us, with all actuality, that we have slowly and laboriously evolved from an appalling silence, chaos and barbarism.

We shall do well, therefore, to wait for no betterment, but to shape our actions as though all that vague instincts and some kind of hereditary optimism promise us were as certain and inevitable as death. The one hypothesis is, after all, quite as probable, quite as unverifiable, as the other: for so long as we remain in our bodies we are almost completely cut off from the spiritual worlds whose existence we presume, and are incapable of communicating with them. In the doubt which assails us, why not choose the hypothesis that is less discouraging? It may, of course, be objected that the hypothesis which hopes for nothing is not necessarily the more discouraging; for we should probably very soon consider a too-confident hope inadequate and become disgusted with it—then we should indeed despair for good and all. Be the truth as it may, "do not let us pretend to alter the nature of things," says Epictetus, "it is neither possible nor useful to make the attempt; but accepting things as they are, let us strive to accord our minds with them." Nearly two thousand years have passed since the disappearance of the philosopher of Nicopolis, and they have brought us nothing more helpful to cling to.

BIBLIOGRAPHY

BIBLIOGRAPHY

H. Smeathman. *Some Account of the Termites which are found in Africa, etc.* (Trans. Roy. Soc., 1781.)

H. A. Hagen. *Monographie der Termiten.* (Linn., Entomolo., Stettin., Vol. X, 1855.)

B. Grassi and A. Sandias. *The Constitution and Development of Termites, etc.* (Quarterly Journal of Microscopic Science. Vol. XXXIX and XL, London.)

G. D. Haviland. *Observations on Termites.* (J. Linn. Soc. Zool., 1898, XXVI.)

Ch. Lespès. *Mémoire sur le termite Lucifuge.* (An. des sciences nat., t. V.)

Filippo Silvestri. *Note preliminari. s. Termitidi e Termitofili sud-americani.* (Bol. Zool., ed. Anat. comp., No. 419, Vol. XVII, 1902.)

Y. Sjöstedt. *Monographie der Termiten Africas.* (K. Svenska vet. Handl., 1900, XXXIV.)

W. W. Froggatt. *Australian Termitidæ.* (Proc. Linn. Soc. N. Wales, 1895, 96–97.)

W. Savile-Kent. *The Naturalist in Australia.* (London, t. IV, 1897.)

Fritz Müller. *Contributions towards the Nat. Hist. of the Termites.* (An. Mag. Nat. Hist., Vol. XIII, 1874.)

Fritz Müller. *Beitrage zur Kenntniss der Termiten.* (Jenaische Zeit. nat., 1873, 75–87.)

Fritz Müller. *Recent Researches on Termites and Honey Bees.* (Nat. Febr., 19, B. 9, 1874.)

E. Wasmann, S.J. *Einige neue Termiten aus Ceyland, Madagascar.* (Ent. Zeit., XII, Wien, 1893.)

E. Wasmann, S.J. *Die Ameisen und Termiten Gaste von Brasilien.* (Verh. d. Zool. Bot. Gesel., Wien, 1896.)

E. Wasmann, S.J. *Neue Termitophilen und Termiten aus India.* (Ann. Mus. Geneva, XXXVI, 1896.)

G. R. OSTEN-SACKEN. *Obser. on Termites found in California.* (Proc. Boston, Soc. XIX, 1877.)

P. H. DUDLEY and J. BEAUMONT. *Observations on the Termites or White Ants of the Isthmus of Panama.* (Trans. New York Acad. of Science, Vol. VII, 1887.)

HG. HUBBARD. *Notes on the Tree Nests of Termites in Jamaica.* (Proc. Post. Soc., XIX, 1878.)

MAYNARD. *Notes on the White Ants in the Bahamas.* (Psyche, V, 1888.)

DR. PACKARD. *Notes on the External Anatomy.* (Third Report, U. S. Entom. Comm., 1883.)

H. McE. KNOWER. *The Development of the Termites.* (Johns Hopkins University Circulars, Vol. XII, No. 126, 1883.)

J. D. E. SCHMELZ. *Ueber Termiten und Termitenbauten.* (Verh. V. F. Nat., Unterhaltung Hamburg, II, 1875.)

CH. DARWIN. *Recent Researches on Termites and Stingless Honey Bees.* (Amer. Nat., VIII, 1874.)

T. J. SAVAGE. *Annals and Magazine of Natural History.* (1850.)

A. DE QUATREFAGES. *Souvenirs d'un Naturaliste.* (Rev. des Deux-Mondes, 1853.)

T. PETCH, 1906. *The Fungi of certain Termite Nests.* (Ann. Roy. Botan. Garden Peradenya, 3: 185–270.)

J. PETCH. *Insects and Fungi.* (Scien. and Progress, Oct. 1907.)

E. HEGH. *Les Termites.* (Bruxelles, 1922.)

H. W. BATES. *Naturalist on the River Amazon.* (London, 1863, and Proc. Linn. Soc., Vol. II, 1854.)

H. G. FORBES. *A Naturalist's Wanderings in the Eastern Archipelago.*

DAVID LIVINGSTONE. *Missionary Travels and Researches in South Africa.* (1857.)

E. BUGNION. *La guerre des fourmis et des termites, etc.* (Geneve, Librairie Kundig, 1923.)

E. BUGNION. *Observations sur les termites. Différenciation des castes.* (Comp. rend. Soc. Biol., Paris, 1, 1091–94.)

E. BUGNION. *La Différenciation des castes chez les termites.* (Bull. Soc. Entom., France, 213–18.)

DR. IMMS. *On the Structure and Biology of Archotermopsis.*

KURT VON ROSEN. *Die fossilen Termiten.* (Transact. Second Entom. Congress, 1912.)

L. R. CLEVELAND. *Symbiosis among Animals, with special reference
to Termites and their Intestinal Flagellates.* (Quat. Rev. of
Zoöl., Vol. I, No. 1, January 1926.)

L. R. CLEVELAND, 1923. *Correlation between the Food and Mor-
phology of Termites and the presence of Intestinal Protozoa.*
(Amer. Journ. Hyg., 3, 444–461.)

L. R. CLEVELAND, 1924. *The Physiological and Symbiotic Relation-
ships between the Intestinal Protozoa of Termites and their
Host, with special reference to Reticulitermes flavipes Kollar.*
(Biol. Bull., 46, 177–225.)

L. R. CLEVELAND, 1925a. *The Ability of Termites to Live perhaps
indefinitely on a Diet of Pure Cellulose.* (Biol. Bull., 48, 289,
293.)

L. R. CLEVELAND, 1925b. *The Effects of Oxygenation and Starvation on the Symbiosis between the Termite, Termopsis, and its
Intestinal Flagellates.* (Biol. Bull., 48, 309–327.)

L. R. CLEVELAND, 1925c. *The Tosicity of Oxygen for Protozoa in
vivo and vitro: Animals Defaunated without Injury.* (Biol.
Bull., 48, 455–468.)

L. R. CLEVELAND. *The Method by which Trichonympha Campanula, a Protozoan in the Intestine of Termites, ingests Solid
Particles of Wood for Food.* (Biol. Bull., April, 1925.)

ANT. DE BARY, 1879. *Die Erscheinung der Symbiose.*

F. DOFLEIN, 1906. *Die Pilzkulturen der Termiten.* (Verhandl. d.
Deutsch. Zool. Ges., 15, 140–149.)

C. FULLER, 1920. *Annals Natal Museum,* 4, 235–295.

C. FULLER, 1921. *The Fungus Food of Certain Termites, S. Afr.*
(Journ. Nat. His., 3, 139–144.)

H. PRELL. *Biologische Beobachtungen an Termiten und Ameisen.*
(Zool. Anz. Marburg. B. 38, Nos. 9 and 10, Sept. 1911.)

N. HOLMGREN. *Studien uber sudamerikanische termiten.* (Zool.
Jarhrb. Abt. System XXIII, 1906.)

N. HOLMGREN. *Termitenstudien.* (Upsala and Stockholm, 1909–
1912.)

J. DESNEUX. *Termites du Sahara.* (Alger. Ann. Soc. entom. Belge,

XLVI, 1902.)

K. ESCHERICH. *Eine Ferienreise nach Erythrea.* (Leipzig, 1908.)

K. ESCHERICH. *Aus dem Leben der Termiten oder weissen Ameisen.* (Leipzig III, Zeit V, 24, 1908.)

K. ESCHERICH. *Die Termiten oder weissen Ameisen. Eine biologische Studie.* (Werna-Klinkhardt Leipzig, 1909.)

K. ESCHERICH. *Termiten auf Ceylon, etc.* (Fischer, Iena, 1911.)

DR. J. BEQUAERT. *Termites du Katanga.*

THE END